Utility and Choice in
Social Interaction

Utility and Choice in Social Interaction

LYNNE OFSHE

University of California at Berkeley

RICHARD OFSHE

University of California at Berkeley

PRENTICE-HALL, INC., *Englewood Cliffs, New Jersey*

PRENTICE-HALL SERIES IN GENERAL SOCIOLOGY
Neil J. Smelser, editor

Current printing (last digit):

10 9 8 7 6 5 4 3 2 1

13-939645-4

Library of Congress catalog card number:
70-101539

Printed in the United States of America

Prentice-Hall International, Inc., *London*
Prentice-Hall of Australia, Pty. Ltd., *Sydney*
Prentice-Hall of Canada, Ltd., *Toronto*
Prentice-Hall of India Private Ltd., *New Delhi*
Prentice-Hall of Japan, Inc., *Tokyo*

PH 2-6-80

Preface

This book is the product of a complex division of labor from start to finish. There was no simple assignment of tasks that could easily be specified. We share equal responsibility for conceptualization, design, execution, analysis, and writing. Whatever strong points exist in the work that are not attributable to Siegel's basic research result from our interaction. Neither one of us could have produced this book alone.

A number of individuals provided help in different fashions at various points in the work. We wish to thank Joseph Berger, Arthur Stinchcombe, Alberta Siegel, and Hamit Fisek for their continual interest and perceptive criticisms, and R. Duncan Luce for commenting on an early draft of the manuscript. We are indebted to Bernhardt Lieberman, Alberta Siegel, Gerald Shure, and Ralph Meeker for providing us with data from their researches. In the execution of the experiments we were aided magnificently by John Messer. The drudgery of typing, retyping, and putting the manuscript into the English language fell to Jeanne Messer; we are truly thankful for her help.

Special mention must be given to the advantages we enjoyed due to the research facilities at our disposal. The experiments were conducted in the Management Science Laboratory of the Center for Research in Management

Science at the University of California (Berkeley). The facility was built with funds provided by the National Science Foundation and the University of California. This highly flexible, computer-based research facility provided an ideal environment in which to work. The analysis of the results of experiments was carried out through the Computation Center of Stanford University. For reasons that were independent of this research project we had at our disposal in San Francisco a remote terminal for the Stanford time-shared IBM 360/67. The power of the Stanford Computation Center's time-sharing and remote-batch-processing systems made computation and data analysis a pleasant experience.

We operated in the best of all possible worlds: with the behavioral science research facilities available at Berkeley and the computation facilities available at Stanford. Had the situation been reversed, it probably would have taken a decade to carry out the research program.

Funds for the researches were provided by the National Science Foundation (G.S. 2152), Stanford University, and the Committee on Research of the University of California (Berkeley).

San Francisco   LYNNE OFSHE
                                                                              RICHARD OFSHE

Contents

Utility and Choice in
Social Interaction

1

Introduction

The generality of a theory is typically calculated in terms of the number and importance of the phenomena that can be explained when its axioms are coordinated to variables operating in concrete situations, and by the number of "middle-range" theories that can be treated as its special cases. Given these criteria, it is obvious that a viable theory of decision making would rank as a highly general formulation and would therefore provide a powerful explanatory device for the analysis of human behavior. Recognition of the importance of the phenomenon as a problem for investigation is reflected by the fact that a substantial proportion of the energy expended by social and behavioral scientists can be considered to be either clearly directed at, or can be organized in terms of, attempts to create an explanation of decision making. The amount of attention the problem receives is clearly commensurate with its scientific status.

That a theory of *human* decision making is essential to the development of a powerful social science is illustrated by consideration of the work of von Neumann and Morgenstern in their *Theory of Games and Economic Behavior* (1944). Their work addressed the problem of finding "an exact description of the endeavor of the individual to obtain a maximum utility, or, in the

case of the entrepreneur, a maximum of profit from his alternative choices"
(p. 1). Their theory united previously unrelated aspects of mathematics and
economics and proposed an elegant theory for a major facet of human behavior. There is no question that von Neumann and Morgenstern's contribu-
tion to the theoretical literature was of considerable importance. As Luce and
Raiffa (1957) have summarized,

> The achievement of von Neumann and Morgenstern is remarkable:
> In the first major publication on the subject, they formulated a clear
> abstraction from the relatively vague social sciences, having both con-
> siderable breadth and mathematical depth, and they developed an
> elaborate and subtle superstructure with masterful scope (p. 11).

Luce and Raiffa also note that:

> . . . we have the historical fact that many scientists have become dis-
> illusioned with game theory. Initially there was a naïve bandwagon
> feeling that game theory solved innumerable problems of sociology and
> economics, or that it made their solution a practical matter of a few
> years' work (p. 10).

The disenchantment with game theory is not accounted for by the fact
that its mathematical structure has proven inconsistent. The problem is that
it simply does not predict the behavior of individuals in situations in which
their decision making should be explained by the theory. There are at least
three ways to account for the failure of the theory to predict behavior. The
theory's axioms may lead to incorrect predictions, it may be an insufficient
explanation and hence yield incorrect predictions, or the tests to which it was
subjected may not have been conducted under appropriate conditions for
evaluation of the theory. The failure of game theory to predict decision making (and therefore to predict behavior) is held to be accounted for by a combination of the latter two alternatives.

Von Neumann and Morgenstern constructed their theory to predict decision making in situations in which it is assumed "that the aim of all participants in the economic system, consumers as well as entrepreneurs, is money,
or equivalently a single monetary commodity" (p. 8). Given their problem,
constructing a mathematical theory that yields strategies which maximize an
individual's gain, the assumption that actors could be treated as being motivated solely by money was of minor importance and probably made for
convenience. The great disappointment with game theory has come about
primarily because researchers have applied the theory without due regard to
the limitations of the heuristic assumption made by the theorists. It is naïve
for behavioral scientists to believe that individuals are motivated solely by
monetary gain. This assumption is inappropriate when "real life" decisions

are being considered, and it is equally inappropriate for consideration of decision making in even highly rarefied and controlled experimental situations. The mathematics of game theory can be applied once the inputs to the equations are correctly identified. Without such identification, game theory, or any other theory which incorporates a model of human decision making at its foundations, will certainly yield predictions for behavior which do not match the manner in which individuals act.

The general position taken in the following work is that much of human behavior can be analyzed from a decision-making perspective, even though the content, social context, and importance of specific decisions can vary greatly. For example, a decision can be a personal, nonsocial choice, such as which of two cars to buy, or it can involve a social decision, such as which friend to tutor the evening before an exam. The assumption used throughout this work is that, although decisions vary in content, importance, and social context, the abstract principles which guide behavior in these choice situations are basically the same. In all such situations an individual is forced to choose a particular element from a set of alternatives, and it is assumed that he makes his decision in a manner which will maximize his expected utility.

Consider the two choice problems mentioned above. The person buying the car has a choice between two alternatives. Both cars sell for the same price; one has rather luxurious appointments, a great deal of power, but a reputation for having mechanical difficulties. The other is somewhat more spartan and less powerful, but has little likelihood of developing problems requiring expensive and time-consuming repairs. The individual takes these factors into consideration and, depending upon which elements have greater utility to him, he makes his decision. In the second choice problem, an individual who is a very competent mathematics student must choose one of two others to tutor. One of his good friends (male) is having an exam the following day in an introductory math course and asks the individual to tutor him that evening. An extremely attractive girl whom the individual does not know very well, but whom he would like to date, also asks him to tutor her that evening for an exam the following day in a different course. In this case, his decision is social in the sense that it affects not only himself, but also the other individuals involved in the choice situation. In determining which person to help he considers such factors as implications for future interaction, positive and negative sanctions which may result from his choice, and the relative value of spending an evening with a friend or with an attractive girl. It is assumed that in this case also the individual will assess the relative utilities and choose that alternative which has the greatest expected utility. Although the utility considerations in these situations come from very different sources, we believe that the same basic principles guide the behavior in both.

It has been argued that such an approach is tautological and incapable of falsification; that is, if the choice an individual makes is always that choice with the maximum expected utility, then the approach has no predictive value. However, if it is possible to assess the utilities before the decision is made, then this approach loses any tautological overtones. Our aim in this work is to follow this strategy in the analysis of a decision-making problem which occurs in a social context.

Siegel et al. (1964) have analyzed a nonsocial choice situation, the Humphreys' (1939) light-guessing experiment, in this manner. They have attempted "to demonstrate that experimental operations based on a consideration of a psychological construct, utility, lead to predictable choice behavior" (Siegel et al., 1964). Their success in this endeavor indicates that this approach may be fruitful in studying other types of decision making.

The coalition game is an intriguing example of choice behavior in a clearly social situation. The individual is forced to choose between other individuals, and his choice has implications not only for his own outcome, but also for the outcomes of the other players in the game. We will view the coalition game as a setting in which to study social decision making. The goal of this work is to develop and test a predictive, utility-based model of social decision making.

2

Social Choice in the Coalition Game

The coalition game experimental situation has been employed by a number of investigators in order to study a variety of theoretical problems. In this chapter, we argue that a substantial proportion of the research literature can be organized in terms of the concepts of utility and probability and that given this organization it is possible to apply a general utility theory to decision making in the game situation.

The impetus for the current interest in coalitions as an area of social-psychological study can be traced to Simmel's (1950) discussion of the alliance of two against one as one of the possible structures into which a triad may evolve. The early studies in this area, such as those by Mills (1953) and Strodtbeck (1954), were not radically different in their primary focus. An increasing concern with game theory and the similarity between the coalition situation and an *n*-person game has led to the creation of a specific "coalition game" which has become a center of interest in most recent research. This changed emphasis is apparent in Gamson's (1964) review article, in which the earlier "nongame" studies are excluded, by definition, from the area of coalition research. While this shift in focus is not necessarily regrettable, it is unfortunate that the current research has concentrated upon explaining behavior in a specific situation with relatively few attempts to generalize to other processes in the triad, or to similar processes occurring in other situations. Although the following analysis of past coalition research will be restricted to studies conforming to the current definition of the area, the basic goal of our analysis is to consider the process of social choice which, of course, is not bound to the coalition game.

The *coalition game* is an *n*-person mixed-motive game; that is, there are elements of competition in that no outcome satisfies everyone, and there are elements of cooperation in that two or more players must ally in order to win. A typical game employs three players, each of whom is assigned a certain weight or resource on each trial. The players are instructed that on each trial a reward, usually monetary, will be given to the individual, or coalition, controlling the majority of resources. The players are then allowed to form coalitions and divide the reward in any manner that they choose. Variations upon the game include increasing the number of players and adding some additional situational factors which increase the players' interest, but do not change the basic structure.

Although the current focus in coalition studies is on the effect of the distribution of resources on the selection of partners and the subsequent division of rewards, it would seem that an understanding of the two separate and distinct subprocesses, that of choosing partners and that of bargaining over a reward, is logically prior to the current concern. The confusion apparent in the present research on coalitions may partly result from the usual technique of treating these two processes simultaneously. In any concrete situation, there is obviously an interaction effect between the two phenomena, and it would not seem possible to study their combined effects until some understanding is obtained of the independent operation of each process. In fact, lacking a conceptual analysis of these processes and a theory of their interaction, aggregated data from coalition experiments may not appear to have any patterning. If, for example, person *a* in a coalition game finds person *b* to "drive a hard bargain," he may choose person *c* regardless of the resource and reward distribution. Since most explanations of behavior in the game situation consider only factors of resources and rewards, while the data reflect many additional variables, the relationship between the variables of primary interest is usually obscured. We believe this is a direct result of the attempt to treat choice and bargaining simultaneously.

This work is concerned with the first of these processes, that of choosing partners. It will be viewed as an individual decision-making process, in which each of the three players in the game is faced with a series of binary choices; that is, he can choose either of the other two individuals on each trial. The theory of the coalition choice process which will be developed in this book is based on the assumption that an individual will behave as if he is maximizing his expected utility. It will further be assumed that, in the simplest coalition choice situation, an individual's expected utility has three components: the utility of the reward received from a winning coalition, the probability of obtaining the reward associated with each alternative, and the desire for equity in the allocation of the total available rewards among the players. Unfortunately, none of the experiments currently reported in the literature have been designed to evaluate adequately this type of approach. However, there is evidence that these considerations are necessary, and perhaps sufficient, to explain choice behavior in coalition games. The object of the following three sections is to demonstrate that the bulk of the coalition game literature can be organized in terms of the utility components introduced above.

2.1 EFFECT OF REWARD ON CHOICE BEHAVIOR

In general, it has been found that an individual will tend to form that coalition from which he can expect to receive the greater of his two possible rewards. The clearest demonstration of this is a study by Lieberman (1962), in which the division of the reward by a winning coalition was not determined by bargaining, but by an established payoff schedule which was constant for all trials. Using this format, each individual was aware of his payoff from each of his two possible coalitions before making his choice. The rewards were such that two individuals could clearly maximize their return by constantly choosing one another. This maximizing coalition occurred on 70% of the trials.

Unfortunately, other studies have allowed the reward to be divided by bargaining after partners have been chosen, so that it is difficult to determine to what extent subjects choose that coalition which would maximize their return. In general, these studies assign resources, or weights, to the subjects who are instructed that the individual, or coalition, with the greatest amount of resources wins a reward, which, if necessary, will then be divided by bargaining. Two contradictory results have been found about choice and bargaining behavior under these circumstances.

The majority of studies (cf. Gamson, 1961; Vinacke, 1959*b*; Chaney and Vinacke, 1960), the first of which was conducted by Vinacke and Arkoff (1957), found that resources tend to dictate a *parity norm* in the bargaining. That is, individuals tend to divide the reward according to the amount of resources contributed to the coalition. It has been argued that in the case in which any two individuals can combine to form a winning coalition (control a majority of the resources), this division of rewards is inappropriate. Since this work is concerned with choice behavior, the rationality of the subjects in their subsequent bargaining is formally outside the present scope. If, however, it is assumed that in these cases a parity norm operates with regard to the share of the reward that an individual can expect, it is possible to assess whether or not the subject chooses that alternative which will maximize his reward. As Gamson (1964) has explained:

> If a player gets from a coalition his parity price, i.e., an amount proportional to his resources, he gets the most by maximizing the ratio of his resources to the total resources of the coalition. Since his initial resources are the same regardless of which coalition he joins, the lower the total resources, the greater will be his share.

In most cases, the two with the least resources form a coalition, a finding which supports the generalization that an individual tends to choose that coalition which maximizes his reward.

Studies by Vinacke et al. (1966) and Kelley and Arrowood (1960) have, however, produced contradictory results; these researchers report that individuals with the minimum resources do not combine more frequently than by chance. For both studies, it is reasonable to conclude that either through direct instruction or through a learning process, subjects became aware of the meaninglessness of resources. It would, therefore, be expected that since resources are seen as irrelevant, the reward would be split more or less equally. An individual trying to maximize his reward should be indifferent to alternative coalitions. Unfortunately, only Kelley and Arrowood's (1960) study reports the bargaining behavior sufficiently to test this reasoning. In that study, the rewards are divided more equally than the resource-based parity norm would dictate. Consequently, the results of this research can be seen as consistent with the generalization as originally stated.

While these two sets of findings indicate that the interpretation of resources by the subjects affects which coalitions form, it is also clear that given the bargains which a player can expect to strike, these studies support the conclusion that an individual will tend to choose that alternative which maximizes his reward.

2.2 EFFECT OF THE DESIRE FOR EQUITY

A second finding about choice behavior in this situation is related to equity concerns. In order to allocate the rewards more equitably among all the players, individuals will not choose that alternative which maximizes their return.

The study by Lieberman (1962) discussed above gives some indications in this direction. In a situation in which it was clearly to the advantage of two of the players to form a coalition, this did not occur in a sizable minority, 30%, of the trials. If the two players had constantly formed a coalition, the third player would have lost almost all of his initial stake. In post-session interviews many subjects stated that complete exclusion of one participant did not seem fair. It appears that the reward was not large enough to compensate for playing an "unfair" game.

In a group of studies by Vinacke and his associates (Uesugi and Vinacke, 1963; Bond and Vinacke, 1961; Vinacke and Gullickson, 1964; Vinacke, 1959b), it was found that females were oriented more toward "mutual satisfaction of the members of the group than towards the goal of winning itself" (Vinacke and Gullickson, 1964, p. 1228). Uesugi and Vinacke (1963) devised a game to enhance the cooperative aspects evidenced by females, i.e., to increase the pressure for equity, and found that both males and females became less concerned with winning and more concerned with playing fairly. While this group of studies has been primarily concerned with sex differences as an explanation, it seems equally reasonable to view these differences as resulting from differential pressures for equity felt by the players.

Studies (cf. Emerson, 1964; Vinacke, 1959a) in which the cumulative scores of the players are displayed during the game show that the players with the lower scores tend to combine. This again indicates an attempt to maintain some type of equality. Kalisch et al. (1954) report a desire on the part of the players to avoid producing a consistent loser. Some studies (cf. Stryker and Psathas, 1960; Vinacke, 1959b) report that players frequently advised others on their best strategy even if this strategy was to the adviser's disadvantage.

No study has concentrated specifically upon this desire for equity; consequently, the findings stated above are necessarily of a somewhat tangential nature. There are, however, consistent indications that the desire for maximization of reward is tempered by a desire for an equitable outcome. Any theory of the choice process must consider both factors, since it would be impossible to exclude the effect of either from an actual experiment.

2.3 EFFECT OF PROBABILISTIC CONSIDERATIONS

Probabilistic aspects of this situation occur in two ways: first, the probability that a player's choice is reciprocated, and second, the probability that the reward is obtained after the coalition has been formed. It is obvious that the latter consideration can be eliminated in the design of the experiment by basing the payoff entirely upon the amount of combined resources. Although this is generally the case, there are some studies in which the receipt of the reward is not completely determined by the resources, but by a probabilistic method. In such studies (cf. Willis, 1962; Chertkoff, 1966), subjects tend to take the relative probability of success into consideration in making their choices. While this factor can be controlled, such a finding indicates that subjects do take probabilistic factors into account.

Unfortunately, the first factor, the probability of reciprocation, has not been controlled and has generally received little attention in current research. One bit of germane information is reported by Gamson (1961). He notes that subjects, in games of more than three players, sometimes chose a coalition which did not maximize their return in order to win more quickly and easily. Chertkoff (1967) reanalyzed Caplow's (1956) theory of coalition formation in light of the question of reciprocation and concluded that this is an important variable in determining which coalitions form. Lack of adequate control in all studies, however, makes it impossible to determine precisely the extent to which the probability of reciprocation influences choice behavior.

Although conclusive evidence on this point is lacking, it seems reasonable to suspect that the probability of reciprocation is a factor influencing the subject's behavior.

3

A Theory and Model
of Decision Making

Although decision making in a coalition situation is much more complex than in a binary choice experiment, certain analogies can be drawn which facilitate the application of findings from more abstract and controlled decision-making research to a social setting. The discussion below presents an analysis of the classic light-guessing experiment. The theory presented here will later be modified for direct application to coalition choice behavior.

3.1 DESCRIPTION OF THE HUMPHREYS' EXPERIMENT

In the Humphreys' (1939) light-guessing experiment, a subject is seated before two bulbs and is instructed to predict which one will illuminate on each of a series of trials. Only one bulb lights on any trial. After his prediction, the subject is able to see whether or not he was correct by simply observing which light subsequently illuminates. The probability that a given bulb will light is fixed in advance and is typically figured for a block of trials. If, for example, the probabilities were .80 and .20 and figured over blocks of

11

20 trials, one light would come on 16 times and the other four times. This allows for examination of process effects by considering the change in the subject's choices over blocks of trials, all of which have the same probability structure. Since one and only one bulb illuminates on each trial, the probabilities corresponding to the lights sum to one.

At the start of this experiment subjects typically distribute their choices equally between the two lights. As the experiment continues, they tend to increase their choices of the more frequently reinforced light. After one to two hundred trials, the behavior of subjects generally stabilizes and they choose each light with the same probability with which the bulb illuminates; this is generally called a *matching strategy*. For example, in the case in which the right light comes on 80% of the time and the left light 20%, the subject will, when he reaches stable-state behavior, distribute his choices with matching percentages; he will choose the right light with a probability of .80 and the left with .20.

If the subject in this experiment wished to maximize the number of correctly chosen lights, his best strategy would be to choose the more frequent event all the time. In this way, in the above example, he would be guaranteed of getting 80% of the choices correct; while, in using a matching strategy, he gets only .80 (.80) + .20 (.20), or 68%, correct. (*Strategy* refers to his distribution of choices, i.e., the probability with which he chooses each light.) Since the usual behavior in the light-guessing experiment is contradictory to a "rational prescription" for maximization of reward, the experiment has generated considerable interest among researchers studying choice and decision making.

3.2 THEORETICAL FRAMEWORK

One theory and model (Siegel et al., 1964) of decision making in the light-guessing experiment is based upon the assumption that the subject behaves as if he is maximizing his expected utility. The term, *utility*, as it is used here does not refer simply to the reward associated with each alternative, but also to any other considerations which may increase the subjective value of a particular choice. In this situation, it is necessary to consider the expected utility of a given choice, since the reward associated with an alternative is realized only if the choice is correct for that trial. Siegel has considered two sources of utility in the light-guessing experiment. The first is the utility of a correct choice, that is, the utility of the reward received for correctly predicting which light will illuminate on a trial. The second source of utility is that of choice variability resulting from the intrinsic boredom of a pure strategy (choosing the same light constantly), as well as from the greater satisfaction connected with being able to predict the less frequent light correctly.

The existence of this latter source of utility is supported by post-experimental interviews with subjects. For example, Siegel and Goldstein[1] found that many subjects realized that a pure strategy would maximize their monetary reward and yet periodically selected the less frequently reinforced light because of the boredom involved in continuously choosing the same light or because of the challenge involved in correctly predicting when the less frequent event would occur. Goodnow (1955) reports that some subjects were able to follow a pure strategy only by inventing games which served to decrease the monotony involved in repeatedly choosing the same alternative. Subjects devised games such as changing the hand used to operate the response key and varying the pressure used in punching the key.

Working on the assumption that the subject is maximizing his expected utility and that this utility stems from two sources, Siegel constructed a formal model of individual choice behavior in this situation. The model predicts the subject's stable-state behavior in a choice situation where the following factors are considered: the probabilities that the choices are reinforced; the marginal utility of a correct choice; and the marginal utility of choice variability.[2] While the model, as derived by Siegel, can apply to any number of alternatives, only the derivation of the two-alternative case will be given here. It should be noted that this model will apply in cases in which the feedback probabilities sum to more, or less, than one; that is, it can be used when neither or both lights are correct on some trials. (For a more complete explanation and a derivation for the *n*-alternative case, see Siegel et al., 1964.)

In deriving the model the following notation will be used:

π_i = the probability that the *i*th light comes on, $i = 1, 2$,

a_i = the marginal utility of a correct choice of the *i*th alternative, $i = 1, 2$,

b = the marginal utility of choice variability, and

P_i = the stable-state probability that the subject chooses the *i*th alternative, $i = 1, 2$.

The purpose of this model is to enable predictions to be made for the subject's stable-state strategy, P_1 and P_2, from the values of the other variables. Employing the concept of mathematical expectation and the above definitions, it is obvious that the expectation that the subject's choice will be correct is

---

1. These feelings are reported in the interview abstracts of the experiment by Siegel and Goldstein (1959). The authors wish to thank Alberta Engvall Siegel for making these abstracts available.

2. *Stable-state choice strategy* refers to an individual's decision strategy after he has "adjusted" to the situation. In choice experiments of the type discussed in this book, it is typically observed that subjects adopt a stable choice strategy after a learning period of variable length. The model is designed to predict only the subjects' stable-state strategies. It is not intended to account for the "adjustment" or "learning" process prior to stabilization.

the sum of the probabilities that he gets each light correct, or $P_1\pi_1 + P_2\pi_2$, and the expected utility of a correct choice is the sum of the expected utilities for all alternatives, or $a_1P_1\pi_1 + a_2P_2\pi_2$. Given the assumption that the utility of choice variability is proportional to the variance of the subject's choice, the interpretation of the utility of choice variability function is quite simple in the case of two alternatives. Assuming that with probability P_1 the subject chooses the first alternative and with probability $P_2 = 1 - P_1$ he chooses the second alternative, it is clear that the model of his choices is that of a sequence of Bernoulli trials (i.e., independent trials) with parameter P_1. Thus the variance of each choice is $P_1(1 - P_1)$, and it is assumed in the model that an individual's utility of choice variability is proportional to the variance of his (random) choice, that is $2bP_1(1 - P_1)$.

The expected utility U of P_1, the stable-state strategy of choosing light one with probability P_1, is assumed to be the sum of these two utility functions:

$$U = a_1P_1\pi_1 + a_2P_2\pi_2 + 2bP_1(1 - P_1)$$
$$= -2bP_1^2 + (a_1\pi_1 - a_2\pi_2 + 2b)P_1 + a_2\pi_2$$

It was assumed that the individual is maximizing his expected utility U by his choice of a strategy, that is, his choice of P_1. The problem is to find the value of P_1 which will maximize U in the above equation. Since U is concave downwards when graphed as a function of P_1, the maximum of U with respect to P_1 occurs when $\partial U/\partial P_1 = 0$:

$$0 = \frac{\partial U}{\partial P_1} = -4bP_1 + a_1\pi_1 - a_2\pi_2 + 2b$$

This equation can be solved for P_1; therefore, the maximum of U occurs when

$$P_1 = \frac{a_1\pi_1 - a_2\pi_2 + 2b}{4b} = \frac{1}{4}\left(\frac{a_1}{b}\pi_1 - \frac{a_2}{b}\pi_2\right) + \frac{1}{2}$$

and substituting α_i for a_i/b:

$$P_1 = \tfrac{1}{4}(\alpha_1\pi_1 - \alpha_2\pi_2) + \tfrac{1}{2} \qquad P_2 = 1 - P_1 \qquad (1)$$

This can be simplified in the case in which the utilities of the two alternatives are equal, that is, $a_1 = a_2(\alpha_1 = \alpha_2 = \alpha)$:

$$P_1 = \tfrac{1}{4}\alpha(\pi_1 - \pi_2) + \tfrac{1}{2} \qquad P_2 = 1 - P_1 \qquad (2)$$

These two sets of equations will predict the stable-state behavior of an individual given the probabilities of feedback and the values of the utilities.[3] It should be noted that in deriving the model, several additional assumptions about the variables have been made; e.g., the expected utility of a choice strategy is the sum of the utilities of correct choice and of choice variability. Such assumptions could be made differently; however, at the present stage of verification there is no indication that any such modifications are necessary.

3.3 TESTS OF THE MODEL IN THE LIGHT-GUESSING EXPERIMENT

Siegel derived and tested several predictions from the model in various situations. Certain ordinal predictions can be made about the effect on the choice strategy of varying the utilities. If the boredom of the pure strategy were decreased, it would predict that the utility of choice variability should be less; the value of b would decrease. The result of this change can be predicted from the model.[4] For example, in the case of equal utilities with $\pi_1 > \pi_2$ and $\pi_1 + \pi_2 = 1$, Eq. (2) becomes $P_1 = \frac{1}{4}(a/b)(2\pi_1 - 1) + \frac{1}{2}$ and $P_2 = 1 - P_1$. Note that $(2\pi_1 - 1)$ is positive since $\pi_1 > \frac{1}{2}$. In the usual experiment, $P_1 = \pi_1$; that is, the subject follows a "matching strategy." If b is decreased, a/b increases and the value of P_1 also increases. This means that the subject should choose the more frequent light with greater than a matching probability. The prediction was tested by conducting two experiments, one

3. It should be noted that with certain combinations of feedback probabilities and utility values, the model can yield predictions for P_i greater than one or less than zero. Since P_i refers to a probability, it is meaningful only between the values of zero and one; consequently, it is necessary to impose a limiting condition on the model (i.e., $0 \le P_i \le 1$) and solve for the maximizing choice strategy within the range of possible values. Since the utility function is monotonically increasing, whenever the model yields a P_i greater than one, it can be shown that the maximizing behavioral strategy is to choose the ith alternative with a probability of one. Analogously, when P_i is less than zero, the maximizing strategy is to choose the ith alternative with a probability of zero.

4. Mathematically, this can be shown by finding the rate of change of P_1 with respect to b, $\partial P_1/\partial b = -(a/4b^2)(\pi_1 - \pi_2)$. If π_1 is greater than π_2, there is an inverse relationship between P_1 and b. Thus, as b decreases, P_1 increases, approaching a pure strategy. The rate of change of P_2 is $\partial P_2/\partial b = (a/4b^2)(\pi_1 - \pi_2)$. Therefore, when π_1 is greater than π_2, P_2 and b are directly related. If π_1 is less than π_2, the relationships of P_1 and P_2 to b are reversed. Note that P_1 and P_2 approach $\frac{1}{2}$ from different directions as b goes to ∞:

$$\lim_{b \to \infty} P_1 = \lim_{b \to \infty} \frac{a}{4b}(\pi_1 - \pi_2) + \frac{1}{2} = \frac{1}{2}$$

$$\lim_{b \to \infty} P_2 = \lim_{b \to \infty} \frac{a}{4b}(\pi_2 - \pi_1) + \frac{1}{2} = \frac{1}{2}$$

Thus, as b increases, the choices tend to become more equally distributed between the two alternatives.

of which involved a more interesting method of choosing lights to decrease the boredom involved; the difference in the stable-state strategies was in the predicted direction.

If the value of making a correct choice were increased, the model would predict that the subject would move closer to the pure strategy, since the value of a is increased while the value of b remains the same. This derivation is obtained in the same manner as the one cited above. Siegel experimentally tested this prediction and found results clearly supporting the model.

The next step in testing the model was to predict the specific numeric values for the choice strategies that subjects would adopt under specified experimental conditions. In order to predict probability values, it was necessary to measure the values of the α ratios. The method used by Siegel to accomplish this had two parts. The first step was to conduct an experiment (or set of experiments in certain cases) with specified payoffs and feedback probabilities. Using the stable-state choice probabilities observed in this (measurement) experiment, the value of α could be found from Eq. (2) above. Theoretically, if the value of α is held constant and the feedback probabilities, π_i, are changed, the maximizing choice strategy will be different. The second step in the procedure for testing the model therefore called for conducting an additional test experiment in which the values of the feedback parameters were changed while the payoffs and boredom inducing aspects of the experiment (that is, the α determining variables) were held constant. The evaluation of the model's predictive power was based on the accuracy with which it could specify in advance the choice strategies adopted by a new group of subjects under the changed experimental conditions.[5]

Siegel conducted a number of tests of the formal model. The first set of investigations consisted of three tests of the model under equal alpha conditions. Since in the notation in the model, α refers to the ratio of the marginal utility of a correct decision to the marginal utility of response variation, situations in which the utility of a correct decision is equal for all alternatives and the utility of response variation is fixed are referred to as *equal alpha conditions*. In this first set of experiments, the utility of a correct choice was equated for both alternatives by assigning the same payoffs to a correct or incorrect prediction of either event. Subjects were paid five cents for every correct prediction and lost five cents every time they made a prediction that failed. This condition was held constant over all experimental treatments. The only differences between treatment conditions were in the probabilities with which the two events occurred. Table 3.1 summarizes the formal charac-

---

5. The procedure used to estimate the alpha ratios and the manner in which predictions are generated will be discussed in detail in the context of the coalition game research reported below. In evaluating Siegel's research it should be remembered that the procedure devised for testing the model was in no sense circular since the measurement and test conditions were completely independent.

Table 3.1 *Formal Characteristics of Decision-Making Experiments in a Nonsocial Situation (Equal Alpha Model)*

Treatment	Probabilities of events 1 and 2 π_1	π_2	Payoffs for predictions of Events 1 and 2 a_1	a_2	Number of subjects
Condition A	.75	.25	±5¢	±5¢	17
Condition B	.65	.35	±5¢	±5¢	16
Condition C	.70	.30	±5¢	±5¢	20

teristics of the three treatment conditions; π_1 and π_2 refer to the probabilities with which the two events occur, and a_1 and a_2 denote the payoffs associated with each event.

Table 3.2 summarizes the results of three applications of the model to data resulting from the experiments described in Table 3.1. Under equal alpha test conditions, data from a single measurement condition are sufficient to permit estimation of the alpha ratio and for derivation of predictions for choice behavior in the test condition. That is, in Eq. (2) there are two variables set by the experimenter, π_1 and π_2. One of the other two variables describes the subject's choice behavior, P_1. The other describes his utility ratio, α. For a given experiment with π_1 and π_2 set, we can use an individual's behavior to estimate his utility ratio. Then we can use this utility ratio to predict his behavior in an experiment with different values of π_1 and π_2. Actually Siegel estimated the average α (utility ratio) for one set of subjects, and assumed that another set in a different experiment would have the same average α if sampled from the same population. Since the measurement and test condi-

Table 3.2 *Results of Applications of the Equal Alpha Model to Nonsocial Decision Making*

Measurement experiment(s)	Prediction experiment	π_1 π_2	Observed P_1 and P_2*	Predicted P_1 and P_2	|Discrepancy|
Condition A	Condition B	.65	.753	.758	.005
		.35	.247	.242	
Condition B	Condition A	.75	.929	.922	.007
		.25	.071	.078	
Conditions A and B	Condition C	.70	.862	.842	.020
		.30	.138	.158	

*The calculation of the subjects' observed stable-state choice strategy was based on the last 20 trials of the experiments.

tions are independent there is no reason prohibiting rotation of test and measurement conditions in order to conduct a number of applications of the model. Since the same treatment conditions are rotated through measurement and test condition status, the multiple applications should, however, be regarded as constituting only a single test of the model.

In the first application of the model, Condition A served as the measurement experiment and Condition B as the test experiment.[6] The model predicted that the mean probability of a P_1 choice in Condition B would be .753 and the mean probability of a P_2 choice would be .247. The observed probabilities of these events were .758 and .242. The absolute discrepancy between the predicted and observed choice strategies was .005. In the second application of the model, Condition B was used as the measurement experiment and the stable-state choice strategies of subjects in Condition A were predicted. In this case the model yielded a prediction which was discrepant from the observed choice behavior by only .007. In the third application, both Conditions A and B were used in order to generate an alpha estimate, and predictions were tested in Condition C. For this application, the model predicted to within .020 of the observed stable-state choice strategy adopted by subjects.

Note that there are considerable differences between the choice strategies adopted by subjects in the three conditions. For example, in Condition A the stable-state probability of a prediction of event 1 was .929, and in Condition B it was .753. The change in the values of π_1 and π_2 from Condition A to Condition B was only .10 (in Condition A, π_1 was .75, and in Condition B it was .65; π_2 was changed from .25 to .35). The changes in the structure of the experiment produced a considerable change in the behavior of subjects. The observed difference in the mean values of the probability of a prediction of both events 1 and 2 was .176. For Condition B the model's prediction of the probability with which subjects would select alternative 1 if they were maximizing expected utility was .758, and the probability with which they chose this alternative was .753.

In a second set of tests, the model was applied to a more complex situation in which there were three different events to be predicted and the ratio of the expected utility of a choice to the utility of response variability was not equal for all events. In these experiments, the payoff for prediction of event 1 was ± five cents for correct and incorrect predictions, and the payoff for correct or incorrect predictions of events 2 and 3 was ± one cent. Table 3.3 summarizes the values of the event parameters and the payoffs for predictions in each of the four experiments.

6. The values of the stable-state choice strategies in the equal alpha experiments were calculated using the last twenty trials in each experimental condition. Due to the increased complexity of the unequal alpha experiments (reported below), the last 80 trials of the experiments were used in the calculation of subjects' stable-state choice strategies for applications of the model.

Table 3.3 *Formal Characteristics of Decision-Making Experiments in a Nonsocial Situation (Unequal Alpha Model)*

Treatment	Probabilities of events 1, 2, and 3			Payoffs for predictions of 1, 2, and 3			Number of subjects
	π_1	π_2	π_3	a_1	a_2	a_3	
Condition D	.65	.25	.10	±5¢	±1¢	±1¢	18
Condition E	.75	.20	.05	±5¢	±1¢	±1¢	18
Condition F	.70	.15	.15	±5¢	±1¢	±1¢	18
Condition G	.70	.50	.40	±5¢	±1¢	±1¢	18

In testing the model, any three of the treatment conditions can be used to perform the measurements necessary to make predictions for subject behavior in the fourth experiment. Table 3.4 presents a summary of the results of the four possible applications of the model. It is clear that the model again proves to be an extraordinarily powerful predictor of behavior. For example, when Conditions D, E, and F are used to estimate the alphas, the absolute discrepancies between the predicted and observed choice strategies adopted by subjects in Condition G are $P_1 = .034$, $P_2 = .009$, and $P_3 = .029$. When the results of all the tests of the unequal alpha version of the model are considered,

Table 3.4 *Results of Applications of the Unequal Alpha Model to Nonsocial Decision Making*

Measurement experiments	Prediction experiment	π_1 π_2 π_3	Observed $P_1, P_2,$ and P_3*	Predicted $P_1, P_2,$ and P_3	|Discrepancy|
Conditions E, F, and G	D	.65	.785	.819	.034
		.25	.119	.110	.009
		.10	.096	.170	.029
Conditions D, G, and F	E	.75	.891	.895	.004
		.20	.076	.068	.008
		.05	.033	.037	.004
Conditions D, E, and G	F	.70	.876	.842	.034
		.15	.058	.079	.021
		.15	.066	.079	.013
Conditions D, E, and F	G	.70	.891	.895	.004
		.50	.076	.068	.008
		.40	.033	.037	.004

*The calculation of the subjects' stable-state choice strategy was based on data from the last 80 trials of the experiments. The selection of the stabilization point was based on inspection of the process data from the experiments (see Siegel et. al, 1964, pp. 125-31).

the average absolute discrepancy between observed and predicted choice strategies is only .016.

The choice model developed by Siegel and his associates was based on a theory which incorporated the assumptions that individuals act so as to maximize expected utility in their decision making and that the utilities from different sources were additive. The formal model of the theory was subjected to intensive testing and was proven to be a powerful predictor of human decision making.

3.4 CONDITIONS FOR APPLICATION OF THE MODEL TO BINARY CHOICE PROBLEMS

This model can be applied to any binary choice situation in which the following conditions are met. First, obviously, the individual must be faced with a series of binary choices, in which one, or both, or none of the alternatives may be correct on each trial. In addition, the correctness of the choices is determined by a probability function which is constant for each alternative and is figured over blocks of trials. Finally, there must be two and only two sources of utility, one stemming from a correct choice and one coming from the desire of the subject to vary his choices. The utility of a correct choice need not be the same for both alternatives. The model predicts that the subject's stable-state behavior will be a result of the feedback probabilities, the utility of a correct choice, and the utility of response variability.

Siegel's work in this area shows that it is possible to formulate a precise mathematical model using utility considerations and that such a model can have predictive power. With the restricted range of parameter values for which the model has been tested, it proved extremely accurate. In the following chapter this theory and model will be utilized in analyzing the coalition choice process.

4

Analysis and Model of Social Choice

In the preceding chapters two separate lines of research have been discussed. The first of these, dealing with the coalition game, considers a complex interactive situation involving two separate processes (bargaining and choice behavior) and some interaction between the two. When the bargaining aspects of the game are eliminated, it becomes apparent that the situation involves three individuals, each of whom is faced with a series of binary decisions. We have assumed that recourse to three basic utility components is sufficient to build a model of decision making in this type of social situation. The second area of research, choice behavior in the light-guessing experiments, was discussed in Chapter 3. At this point, Siegel's theory and model of decision making in this experiment were introduced. The theory was based upon the assumption that an individual in a choice situation will behave as if he is maximizing his expected utility. By determining the utility functions in the situation and applying the above assumption, Siegel constructed a model of choice behavior which appears to have great power. These two apparently disparate lines of research may be joined when one realizes that both are dealing with the same basic problem, that of individual decision making.

Given the assumption that all decision making is guided by an abstract set of axioms which vary only in the manner in which they are operationalized in substantive situations, it is possible to apply the basic concepts of Siegel's model to any concrete decision-making problem. The purpose of this chapter is to describe how this strategy can be employed in constructing a theory of choice behavior in the coalition situation. Fortunately, this application is greatly simplified by the fact that it is possible to consider the utility components involved in the coalition choice process as directly analogous to those considered by Siegel in the light-guessing experiment. It should be pointed out that after elements of a choice situation have been translated into utility components and combined, the particular source of utility becomes irrelevant. For example, money and positive sanctions could be interchangeable in a theory based on utility factors, if both have the same effect (excluding magnitude of effect) on choice behavior. Consequently, although the substantive considerations are somewhat different between the coalition choice problem and the light-guessing experiment, the same set of operational definitions is applicable.

4.1 A THEORY OF THE COALITION CHOICE PROCESS

We assume that choice behavior in the coalition situation is affected by three factors: the probability of reciprocation; the rewards associated with each alternative; and the equity considerations. We postulate that these factors operate in the same manner as the three factors affecting behavior in the light-guessing experiment: the probability of a correct choice; the payoffs associated with each alternative; and the basic monotony of the situation.

In a coalition game, an individual can win a reward only if his choice is reciprocated. This directly corresponds to a correct prediction in the light-guessing experiment; an individual receives a payoff only if the light which he has chosen subsequently illuminates. Thus, it is obvious that a reciprocated choice in the coalition game is strictly analogous to a correct choice in the light-guessing experiment. Letting

a_i = the marginal utility of a reciprocated choice with participant i,
  $i = 1, 2$,
P_i = the stable state probability that the player chooses participant i,
  $i = 1, 2$, and
π_i = the probability that the player is chosen by participant i, $i = 1, 2$,

the expected utility of a reciprocated choice is $\pi_1 P_1 a_1 + \pi_2 P_2 a_2$. This function employs the same implicit assumptions which Siegel used in analyzing the light-guessing experiment.

The second utility considered in the light-guessing situation, the utility of choice variability, may not seem to apply in this situation, for it could be argued that the game itself destroys boredom as well as any desire to choose the less frequently reinforced alternative. However, there is a factor in this situation which is not operating in the light-guessing experiment. Each time an individual forms a coalition, the other person is rewarded as well as himself. This means that if two players constantly form a coalition, the third player receives nothing. There is evidence that an equity norm causes a utility of choice variability. Lieberman (1962) points out that the results of one of his experiments "describe the behavior of three individuals in a situation where two have a clear incentive to unite forces to the detriment of the third. In a majority of choices [70%] the two did just that. However, in a sizable minority of choices [30%] this prescribed behavior did not occur.... Some subjects felt it was not fair to do this" (p. 218). Since this equity norm results in a subjective utility in varying choices, it is directly comparable to the utility of choice variability in the light-guessing experiment. Thus, letting

b = the marginal utility of choice variability,

the equations for the player's behavior can be derived in exactly the same manner as in Siegel's decision-making model for the light-guessing situation. Therefore, the following equations should describe an individual's choice behavior in the coalition game:

$$P_1 = \tfrac{1}{4}(\alpha_1 \pi_1 - \alpha_2 \pi_2) + \tfrac{1}{2}$$
$$P_2 = 1 - P_1$$
(unequal payoffs)

$$P_1 = \frac{\alpha}{4}(\pi_1 - \pi_2) + \tfrac{1}{2}$$
$$P_2 = 1 - P_1$$
(equal payoffs)

The assumptions employed in constructing this model are similar to those used by Siegel in his model for the light-guessing experiment; the only changes are in the substantive interpretation of certain variables.

In the light-guessing situation the subject's behavior stabilizes at a certain level. This level parallels the level at which the lights are reinforced, and the difference between the probabilities of choosing each alternative is a function of the utilities involved. The assumption that an individual in a perceived interactive situation will also stabilize in the same manner seems on first

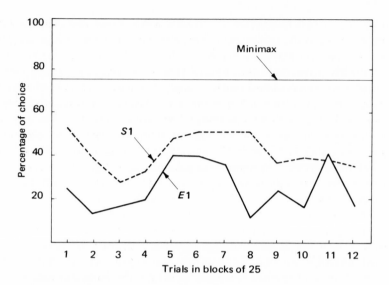

Figure 4.1 *Behavior in a Two-Person Matrix Game (I).* Choices of *S*1 by the subject and *E*1 by the experimenter in game in which experimenter chose *E*1 with probability of .25 (unblocked).

inspection to be tenuous; however, the results of the following study in a two-person situation give support to this type of approach.

Lieberman (1962) reports results of an experimental two-person game in which subjects were presented with the following payoff matrix:[1]

$$
\begin{array}{ccc}
 & E1 & E2 \\
S1 & +3 & -1 \\
S2 & -9 & +3 \\
\end{array}
$$

The rows indicate the subject's choices, and the columns indicate the choices of the other person; the numbers in the cells represent the subject's monetary payoff. For example, if the subject chooses *S*1 and the other person chooses *E*1, the subject receives three cents.

Although the subject was led to believe that he was actually playing against a human opponent, the choices of his opponent were pre-set by the experimenter. The purpose of the experiment was to test a game theory prescription for behavior. The hypothesis was that the subject should choose alternative *S*1 with a probability of .75 and *S*2 with a probability of .25. In the experiment, the choices of the other person were set by the experimenter with the probability of *E*1 at .25 and the probability of *E*2 at .75. It should be noted that the probability was figured over the entire 300 trials; thus, for any

1. The authors wish to thank Berthardt Lieberman for making this data available.

25 trials, the actual number of *E*1 choices made could vary considerably. Figure 4.1 presents the choices by the experimenter and subject for the alternatives *E*1 and *S*1. The game theory prediction obviously failed; however, the results are pertinent to the concern here. The curves match very closely except that the subject consistently chooses alternative *S*1 somewhat more frequently than the experimenter chooses *E*1. Notice that when the subject chooses *S*1, he can lose only one cent, while with a choice of *S*2 he can lose nine cents. It would seem that the utilities of the two responses differ since the gain associated with each is the same while the loss for one of the choices is considerably greater. In light of Siegel's model, it does not seem unreasonable to predict that the subject would choose the alternative with the lower loss somewhat more frequently than with a matching probability, and this is precisely what happens.

In a slightly modified version of the same game, the results were very similar. This game is particularly interesting because the experimenter changed his behavior after the first 100 trials. For the first third of the experiment, the experimenter behaved as before, choosing *E*1 with a probability of .75 and *E*2 with a probability of .25. For the last 200 trials, the experimenter chose each alternative 50% of the time. The subject's behavior (see Figure 4.2) reflects this change in the experimenter's behavior. The experimenter's behavior changed in the fifth block of 25 trials. Observe that subjects shift their behavior and adjust to the experimenter's new strategy almost immediately. Of particular importance is the fact that the subjects in both

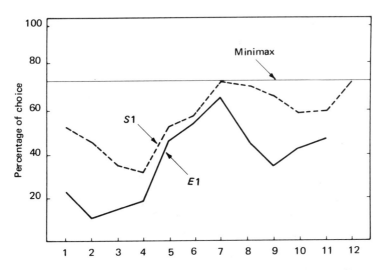

Figure 4.2 *Behavior in a Two-Person Matrix Game (II).* Choices of *S*1 by the subject and *E*1 by the experimenter in game in which experimenter chose *E*1 with probability of .5 (unblocked) on the final 200 trials.

games felt that they were actually playing against an opponent who was taking their responses into account.

Since the probabilities of feedback in this study were not blocked, the comparison of results to those of the light-guessing situation is not entirely valid. However, in such a comparison, the most striking element is the apparent lack of a prolonged learning period in this supposedly interactive game. The subject seems to immediately adjust his behavior to that of the experimenter. The behavior indicates that Siegel's model, or a similar one, could be used to predict the stable-state behavior in such situations. If there is a relatively immediate adaptation to the feedback probabilities, the model could be very powerful in the analysis of such situations.

4.2 EXTENSION OF THE THEORY TO FREE INTERACTIVE SOCIAL SITUATIONS

As originally constructed by Siegel, the model was designed to predict choice strategies in situations in which the probabilistically determined events were generated by specified probability functions and blocked over series of trials. That is, the probabilities which determined the occurrences of the events that subjects had to predict were predetermined and fixed such that they were constant within trial blocks. In all of Siegel's research testing the model, the condition was always enforced that the probabilities of the events to be predicted were blocked within sets of 20 trials. The basic research testing the viability of the proposed analysis of social decision making in the coalition game and the application of the general theory was carried out under similar conditions (this research is reported in Chapters 5, 6, 7, and 8). In this series of studies, the probabilities with which the subject finds the other players choosing him are determined in advance and blocked over series of trials.

The theory is not, however, limited to situations in which the relevant events in the individual's environment (the behaviors of the other players in the game, etc.) are determined by the researcher. The model can be applied to truly interactive social situations, such as coalition games in which three players are free to choose one another without any control introduced by the experimenter. In a situation of this type, it is within the realm of possibility for players to form permanent coalitions, to actually influence the behavior of the other players in the game or otherwise engage in the range of possibilities open to three individuals who are participating in a free interaction.

The generalization of the model to free interactive situations permits prediction of the behavior of each of the participant individuals. These predictions take account of the fact that three players interact and are affected by the actions of each of the other players. Since the generalization yields predictions for the behavior of each of the members of the interaction system, the final result is prediction of how the system itself will behave. That is, by combining models for the behaviors of each of the members of a group, it is possible to predict the behavior of the group considered as a system.

The accuracy with which the generalization of the model predicts the interaction system depends to some extent on whether or not it is necessary to allow for an extended "learning" period in the application of the model to data generated in highly controlled experiments in which the behaviors of the players supposedly participating with the subject are determined by the researcher. As will be shown in Chapter 7, subjects adapt with relatively great speed to the behaviors of the other players in the game. This indicates that they make relatively little attempt to control the behavior of the others in the situation, but rather adapt their own behaviors to the situation as defined by the other participants. The following section will describe the manner in which the model can be generalized to predict the behavior of systems of freely interacting individuals from knowledge of the utility assignments of the members of the interaction system.

4.3 A MODEL FOR SYSTEMS OF FREELY INTERACTING INDIVIDUALS

The basic form of the model considers the behavior of a single individual in a situation in which three factors are assumed to affect his behavior. The factors are (1) the probability with which he is chosen by the other players, (2) the marginal utility of the payoffs he receives for forming alternative coalitions, and (3) his marginal utility for an equitable distribution of the total payoffs in the game. In order to apply this model, it is necessary to control the probabilities with which the relevant events occur. In the context of the coalition game, this means controlling the probabilities with which the individual is chosen by each of the other participants. Compare this situation to a three-person interaction system in which each individual is free to choose either of the other players. These two situations need differ only with regard to the probabilities with which an individual is chosen by each of the other players. That is, the experimenter no longer controls this component. The payoffs for forming alternative coalitions and the equity inducing aspects of the game can be easily held constant across the two game situations. The behavior of the three separate individuals, 1, 2, and 3, can be described by the following equations of the basic model:

$$P_{1,2} = \tfrac{1}{4}(\alpha_{1,2}\pi_{2,1} - \alpha_{1,3}\pi_{3,1}) + \tfrac{1}{2} \qquad P_{1,3} = 1 - P_{1,2}$$

$$P_{2,1} = \tfrac{1}{4}(\alpha_{2,1}\pi_{1,2} - \alpha_{2,3}\pi_{3,2}) + \tfrac{1}{2} \qquad P_{2,3} = 1 - P_{2,1} \qquad (1)$$

$$P_{3,1} = \tfrac{1}{4}(\alpha_{3,1}\pi_{1,3} - \alpha_{3,2}\pi_{2,3}) + \tfrac{1}{2} \qquad P_{3,2} = 1 - P_{3,1}$$

where $P_{x,y}$ is the probability that player x chooses player y, $\pi_{y,x}$ is the probability that player x is chosen by player y, and $\alpha_{x,y}$ is player x's utility ratio for a coalition with player y.

Note that the derivation of predictions for free interactive behavior rests on the ability to determine the probabilities of reciprocation, $\pi_{y,x}$, in such situations. Assume that independent estimates are obtained for all α's in the above set of equations. (These estimates can be obtained experimentally.) The only other term necessary to predict $P_{x,y}$ is $\pi_{y,x}$. The values of $\pi_{y,x}$ can be obtained as follows.

In free interactive situations, $P_{x,y}$ is equal to $\pi_{x,y}$. That is, for any player, say player one, the probability that he chooses player two is obviously identical to the probability that player two is chosen by player one. In any interaction system of the type being considered, the outputs of any one member $(P_{x,y})$ constitute half of the inputs of each of the other members $(\pi_{x,y})$. When all of the outputs of the three players are determined, it follows that all of the inputs for the three players are also determined. In terms of the above example, the notation would be as follows: $P_{1,2} = \pi_{1,2}$, where $P_{1,2}$ is a term in the equation which predicts player one's choice strategy and $\pi_{1,2}$ is a term in the equation for player two's choice strategy. The relations between the P and π values for the three players in a game are as defined below.

$$\pi_{1,2} = P_{1,2} \qquad \pi_{1,3} = 1 - P_{1,2}$$
$$\pi_{2,1} = P_{2,1} \qquad \pi_{2,3} = 1 - P_{2,1} \tag{2}$$
$$\pi_{3,1} = P_{3,1} \qquad \pi_{3,2} = 1 - P_{3,1}$$

Substituting the set of equations above (set number 2) into the basic model's equations for the behavior of each of the three players in a game (set number 1), the following equations are obtained:

$$P_{1,2} = \tfrac{1}{4}(\alpha_{1,2}P_{2,1} - \alpha_{1,3}P_{3,1}) + \tfrac{1}{2}$$
$$P_{2,1} = \tfrac{1}{4}[\alpha_{2,1}P_{1,2} - \alpha_{2,3}(1 - P_{3,1})] + \tfrac{1}{2} \tag{3}$$
$$P_{3,1} = \tfrac{1}{4}[\alpha_{3,1}(1 - P_{1,2}) - \alpha_{3,2}(1 - P_{2,1})] + \tfrac{1}{2}$$

The equations in set number 3 can be arranged as a system of linear equations as follows:

$$4P_{1,2} - \alpha_{1,2}P_{2,1} + \alpha_{1,3}P_{3,1} = 2$$
$$\alpha_{2,1}P_{1,2} - 4P_{2,1} + \alpha_{2,3}P_{3,1} = \alpha_{2,3} - 2 \tag{4}$$
$$\alpha_{3,1}P_{1,2} - \alpha_{3,2}P_{2,1} + 4P_{3,1} = \alpha_{3,1} - \alpha_{3,2} + 2$$

Since the values of the utilities, $\alpha_{x,y}$, are determined independently by experimentation, these three equations can easily be solved for the values of $P_{1,2}$,

$P_{2,1}$, and $P_{3,1}$. The method for estimating the values of the α parameters does not call for using data obtained from subjects whose behavior is then to be predicted.[2] The solutions to the system of equations are somewhat awkward; for example, the probability with which player one chooses player two is given by the following equation:

$$P_{1,2} = \frac{-32 + \alpha_{2,3}\alpha_{3,2}(2 - \alpha_{1,3}) + \alpha_{1,2}\alpha_{2,3}(3 - \alpha_{3,1}) + 8(\alpha_{1,3} - \alpha_{1,2}) + 2\alpha_{1,3}(2\alpha_{3,1} - \alpha_{3,2}) + \alpha_{1,2}(\alpha_{2,3})^2}{-64 + 4\alpha_{2,3}\alpha_{3,2} + 4\alpha_{1,2}\alpha_{2,1} + 4\alpha_{1,3}\alpha_{3,1} - \alpha_{1,2}\alpha_{2,3}\alpha_{3,1} - \alpha_{1,3}\alpha_{3,2}\alpha_{2,1}} \quad (5)$$

However, with values for the alphas, the evaluation of such equations is trivial.

Given that solutions for equations of type (5) are obtained for each of the players in the game, it is obvious that the equilibrium behavior of the interaction system is completely specified. The result of the above generalization of the model is the power to predict the behavior of a group of freely interacting individuals, in a complex social situation, by combining predictions for the behavior of the group's member individuals. The behavior of each group member is itself predicted from a utility-based theory of decision making which postulates that actors can be treated as if they are acting to maximize expected utility in their decision making.

4.4 SUMMARY

The preceding sections presented an analysis of two seemingly disparate lines of research in social psychology and showed that it is theoretically feasible to conceptualize a particularly complex social situation in terms of a general decision-making theory. A review of existing research strongly supported the contention that a model, such as the one proposed above, could be developed in order to explain social choice. The particular decision-making model proposed here appears likely to be a powerful formulation for two reasons. First, it has already been shown to generate extremely accurate predictions for choice behavior in a nonsocial, probabilistic situation. Second, since the setting in which the model was initially tested is structurally analogous to the coalition choice setting, the model may be applied without doing violence to its assumptions.

2. Applications of the basic model and the generalization are made under conditions in which estimates of the alpha constants are obtained from data generated by one set of subjects under specified experimental conditions. Tests of the model's predictive power are made by assessing its ability to predict the behavior of different subjects under substantially changed experimental conditions. The procedure for measurement of the utilities and testing the theory was used by Siegel in his work with the model. It is discussed in detail in Chapter 7.

Although there are substantial reasons to believe that the choice model will work for social decision making, and there is no obviously contradictory evidence known to the present writers, a successful transition from the light-guessing experiment to the coalition setting is by no means guaranteed. The major problem is whether or not the model can handle the greater situational richness of the coalition game. For example, in Siegel's light-guessing experiments, subjects were informed that the behavior of the lights was in no way contingent upon their choices. The pattern of illuminations was fixed prior to the start of the experiment. In the coalition situation, this condition is reversed since each subject believes that the other players will react to his choices. Subjects in the coalition setting must attempt to predict the behavior of two other humans. They can conceivably attempt to influence the others' behaviors, become angry at the other participants, and attempt to apply punishments for disloyalty even at the cost of their own payoffs, or generally engage in a range of behaviors unlikely to occur in the light-guessing experiment.

5

Research Strategy

In the previous chapters, a theory and model of social decision making in the context of the coalition formation game were developed. We argued that in this particular situation three factors affect decision making. Building on certain assumptions about the precise effects of the component factors, the manner in which they combine, and the assumption that individuals in a choice situation act as if they are maximizing their expected utility, we were able to construct a model which allows precise numeric predictions to be made for an individual's choice strategy.

The research reported here constitutes the first step in the evaluation of this theory and model. In order to provide a solid foundation for more extensive research with these formulations, the present effort is concerned with testing the basic tenets of the theory. The decision to begin evaluation of the theory in a relatively uncomplicated research setting was conditioned by the fact that under such circumstances it would be possible to independently test each of the theory's major axioms before attempting predictions utilizing the model. The major advantages of this somewhat conservative research design are that it is possible to (1) unambiguously identify the cause of a failure in prediction if one occurs and (2) guard against acceptance of spurious success as proof of the theory's power.

Theoretically, it would be possible to proceed directly with testing the model by attempting to precisely predict the probabilities of certain behaviors in a complex situation involving factors such as unequal utilities for alternative coalitions and maximum assignment of utility for equity. Unfortunately, this type of strategy results in two possible outcomes, each of which leaves uncertainties with regard to the level of confirmation of the theory's axioms. Given a direct approach, if the predictions of the model prove accurate, there is still no assurance that the accuracy is a result of correctly identifying the appropriate independent variables. That is, one of the independent variables may not be affecting behavior in the hypothesized manner, and because of another unidentified variable, an accidental occurrence, or a fortuitous combination of the three variables, the model could predict accurately. If, on the other hand, the model proved inaccurate given only a direct test, there would be absolutely no available information which could lead to identification of the reason for failure. The formal model proposed in the previous chapter is, after all, only one of a large number of possible formulations which are consistent with the theory. Therefore, a failure of this model does not necessarily mean the axiom structure of the theory needs revision.

Given the uncertainties about results which arise from initial direct tests of the model, the strategy decided upon for this research program was first to test hypotheses following directly from a limited set of axioms and then to test the power of the model to predict behavior precisely.

5.1 RESEARCH DESIGN

The first part of the research, that testing the basic assumptions of the theory, is concerned with the effect of certain independent variables on choice behavior. The hypotheses to be tested are concerned only with establishing that each of three independent variables has a causal effect on choice behavior. The hypotheses are formulated in the classical fashion: as variable x increases, the probability of a choice of a given alternative will increase (or decrease). The hypotheses are concerned with the general effect of the independent variables and do not make precise predictions for the magnitudes of effects. The following three hypotheses are to be tested:

I. As the probability of being chosen by another player increases, the probability of an individual choosing that player increases.

II. As the utility of the payoff received from a coalition increases, the probability of an individual choosing that alternative increases.

III. As an individual becomes more concerned with maintaining equity in the allocation of total available rewards, his choices become more evenly distributed between the other two players.

Each of the three hypotheses stated above specifies the effect of one of the major variables identified by the theory. For example, the theory assumes that, if all other variables are held constant, as the expected utility of a coalition increases, individuals will be more likely to select that coalition. The expected utility of a reciprocated choice is defined as a function of the utility of the payoff for forming a coalition and the probability of being able to enter the coalition. The first two hypotheses specify the separate effects of these two factors. If there is an increase in either the probability of being chosen by a given player, or in the utility of entering a coalition with a player, then the expected utility of that choice increases and, therefore, the likelihood of the individual choosing the coalition increases. The third assumption of the theory is that players in coalition games are more or less concerned with maintaining an equitable distribution of the total rewards among participants in the game. It is assumed that, if all other variables are held constant, as the desire for equity (the individual's utility for equity) increases, individuals will tend to distribute their choices more evenly between the other players in the game.

It was pointed out earlier (in Chapter 2) that the usual coalition game situation involves bargaining as well as choice processes and therefore does not provide a proper setting in which to conduct research on the choice theory. In order to test the proposed formulation, it is necessary to have control over the three independent variables: the utility of the payoffs; the probabilities of being chosen; and the desire for equity. Control over the utility of payoffs can easily be attained since it is generally true that the greater the monetary value of a payoff, the greater the utility of the payoff. By making the difference between payoffs sufficiently large, it is safe to make the assumption that the utilities will differ in the expected direction. Controlling the subjects' desires for equitable division of the total rewards also presents no serious problem. Unfortunately, the third, and perhaps the most important variable, the probabilities with which the subject is chosen by the other players, cannot be strictly controlled in games with three human players.

While there are analytic procedures which may be used in order to obtain partial control over these probabilities when three human players interact, the simplest and most straightforward fashion in which to control the probabilities is to simulate the behavior of two of the three players in a game. That is, to construct a situation in which each subject believes that he is playing against two other individuals, but in reality would be seeing choices made by robot players whose behavior was predetermined by the experimenter. In this way, it is possible to attain complete and precise control over the probability of being chosen by each of the other players.

A test situation was designed which permitted control over the three crucial variables. The situation is described below.

5.2 PROCEDURES

The experimental situation incorporates the necessary components for testing the theoretic approach while eliminating the factors which would tend to mask the causal relations between variables. Each subject is faced with a choice between two players, each of whom chooses him at a specified probability level. Although he believes that he is taking part in a three-person game, he is actually playing with two simulated players whose behavior is predetermined by the experimenter. The subject is aware of his monetary payoff from each of his two possible coalitions, and these rewards are the same for all iterations of the game. The subject is not aware of the payoffs which the other players are receiving from their possible coalitions. In addition, he knows that all three players are of the same sex, although he does not know the exact identity of the other participants in his game.

The research was conducted in a computerized, man-machine laboratory operated by the Center for Research in Management Science at the University of California, Berkeley. The physical setup of the laboratory for this research utilized one large room for the group instructions and nine small rooms for the actual playing of the game. The large room contained chairs, a table, and a blackboard. After the instructions were completed, the subjects were taken to the smaller rooms to play the game. Each of these rooms contained a chair and a teletype. On each iteration of the game, information about the choices of the simulated players and his own winnings was given to the subject via his teletype. The nine teletypes were controlled by a PDP-5 computer programmed with an in-house time-sharing system. The computer was in a back room and never seen by the participants.

The subjects were volunteers from undergraduate sociology courses being given at the university. At the time that they volunteered they were aware of the following factors relating to the experiment. First, they knew that several other students would be present for the same experimental session. Second, they were told that since several studies were being conducted, the amount of payment varied; however, they could expect to be paid approximately $2 per hour for their time. Finally, they were aware that the usual study lasted about one hour.

Subjects were scheduled in groups of nine. If some subjects did not appear at the appointed time, confederates were used to fill in during the instruction period in order to bring the total number of apparent players to six, or nine. After all the subjects (and confederates) had been seated in the large room, the following instructions were read by the experimenter:[1]

1. For brevity, the segments of the instructions dealing with the operation of the teletype have been deleted. Except for this omission, the instructions report everything that was told to the subjects.

In today's session, we are studying an aspect of group interaction. You will be taking part in what is called a coalition game. This game is played by groups of three individuals. Since there are nine (six) of you here today, there will be three (two) separate games, with three of you participating in each game. A game consists of a series of plays; on each play, every participant is asked to choose one of the other players as a coalition partner. If two persons select each other as partners, they have formed a coalition and each of them receives a reward in the form of money; the third person receives nothing. You can win only by forming a coalition. It is possible that on some plays, no one will win. This occurs when no player's choice has been reciprocated. Consequently, on each play, at most two persons can win a reward, and at least one person must lose. Your object is to win as much money as you can.

From a single player's viewpoint, the game is very simple. On each play, you must choose one of the other two participants as a partner. If the person you have selected has also chosen you, you have formed a coalition and consequently win a reward. From your viewpoint, there are four possible outcomes to a play. Assume that you are player one. You may form a coalition with either player two or player three. In both cases, you would win a reward. Players two and three may choose one another; in this case, because you are not in a coalition, you would win nothing regardless of whom you had chosen. Finally, no coalition may form; this occurs when no player's choice is reciprocated and in this situation, none of the players will win anything. Since you can win a reward only if the person whom you have chosen has also selected you, you should try to predict which of the other players are going to choose you on each trial.

In this game you and the other two players will not communicate verbally but through teletypes which are connected together. The teletypes are set up so that you will *not* necessarily be playing with the persons in the immediately adjoining rooms. For example, the player in this room (experimenter points) might be connected with a player in the room down there (experimenter points) and another player over here (experimenter points). When we have completed the instructions you will each be taken to a smaller room in which you will find a teletype. Posted on the teletype will be your player number and information about the reward that you will receive from each of your two possible coalitions.

(The next three paragraphs discussed the use of the teletype equipment.)

Before you begin playing, let's summarize the main points. You'll be playing a coalition game with two other players. On each play, each of you will choose one of the other two players for a coalition partner. After all of you have made your choices, you will be able to see which of the others has chosen you. If the person whom you have chosen has also chosen you, you will win a monetary reward. Remember that your object is to win as much as you can. You can win a reward only if the person whom you have chosen has also selected you, so you should try to predict which of the others are going to choose you on each play. You should be concerned only *with winning as much as you possibly can.*

The above instructions were used in all conditions except those which required increasing the desire for equity. In these conditions, certain changes in the instructions were made in order to induce subjects to assign a greater utility to maintaining an equitable distribution of rewards. The specific changes will be discussed when the equity experiments are reported.

After the instructions were finished, the subjects were taken individually to the smaller rooms. Each subject was shown where certain keys were located on the teletype. Posted on his teletype was a sheet which informed him of the payoffs for entering each of his two possible coalitions. The subject was verbally informed of his alternative payoffs by the experimenter. The experimenter pointed out that these payoffs were specified on the instruction sheet attached to the teletype. The sheet was left on the teletype during the play of the game in case subjects needed to refresh their memories about payoffs for alternative coalitions. When the subject was informed of his payoffs, he was made aware of the fact that he had no information about, and therefore no basis for making any inferences about, the payoffs that the other players were receiving for forming coalitions with him. Each subject was told that the other players might be getting the same amount, more, or less money for forming coalitions with him than he was receiving for forming coalitions with them. If, for example, the subject were told that he would receive five cents each time he formed a coalition with player X, it was made clear to him that player X could be receiving any amount of money for a coalition with the subject.

After all the subjects were in the smaller rooms, the experiment began. Following transmission (via teletype) of an instruction to begin, subjects typed their first names on the teletype and were then led through some simple demonstrations of the equipment. First, they were asked to separately choose each of the other players in the game. The purpose of these demonstrations was to allow the subject to become accustomed to the operation of the teletype prior to the actual start of the game.

Each subject believed that he was player number three in the game. The player number was simply an identifier and indicated nothing about order of response or anything else. Each subject was faced with choosing to attempt to form a coalition with either player number one or player number two. The behavior of these players was simulated. Each of the robot players chose the subject at a specified probability level. For example, player one might choose the subject 70% of the time and player two, 50%.[2] The probabilities with which the simulated players chose the subject were blocked over each set of 10 successive trials. For the above example, the subject would be chosen seven times by player number one and five times by player number two in each 10-trial block. Naturally, on some trials he would be chosen by both players and on some trials chosen by neither. The experiment consisted of 100 iterations of the game. The choices of the simulated players were stored in the computer and were the same for all subjects in a given treatment condition.

On each iteration of the game there was a variable time delay between the point at which the subject made his choice and his subsequent receipt of information about the outcome of the trial. This delay was introduced in order to reinforce the illusion that the other players in the game were humans whose decision times might vary.

After each trial, subjects were informed of the outcome of the play. This was accomplished by sending to the subject, via the teletype, one of four possible messages. The subject (player number three) in a game in which there was a five cent payoff for forming either coalition would receive a message in which he was informed as to who chose him and whether or not he won anything on that trial. The segment of the message that concerned the choices of the other players was fixed prior to the start of the experiment. The segment of the message relating to the payoff varied depending upon the subject's actual choice. If player X was scheduled to choose the subject, and the subject had chosen player X, the message informed the subject that he had won the payoff. If under these conditions he had chosen player Y, he was informed that he had won nothing. Subjects received one of the following four messages after each iteration of the game:

1. You were chosen by player one. You won (five cents or nothing).
2. You were chosen by player two. You won (five cents or nothing).
3. You were chosen by players one and two. You won five cents.
4. You were chosen by no one. You won nothing.

Each subject was handled separately by the computer and could therefore proceed at his own rate. Subjects generally finished the series within about five minutes of one another. The actual play of the game took approximately 35 minutes.

When each subject finished the series he was given a questionnaire. The questionnaire included items concerning his perception of the research, his

2. The numbers of the simulated players were counterbalanced; that is, for half the subjects, player one chose him with the higher probability, and for half the subjects, player two chose him with the higher probability.

impressions of the other players, and questions about various aspects of his behavior. After the subject completed the questionnaire he was taken back to the large room. When all the subjects had finished, the purpose of the research was explained in detail, and all questions about the study were answered.[3] Participants were then paid two dollars for their time.[4]

All of the experiments reported in the following chapters were conducted in this setting. The only change between experimental and control conditions was in the value of the particular independent variable whose effect was being tested: either the probability of being chosen, the payoff for forming a coalition, or the desire for an equitable distribution of the total available rewards.

3. The questionnaire included items designed to uncover suspicion. In the debriefing session, subjects were also given an opportunity to indicate that they had been suspicious during the experiment. No subjects indicated a sufficiently clear case of suspicion to warrant being dropped from the analysis. Except in the cases of two subjects who were unable to complete the session due to equipment failure, the analysis of results for each experiment is based on the data from all subjects who began that experiment.

4. Since subjects were randomly assigned to treatment conditions designed to vary certain utility and reward factors, some subjects were accidentally disadvantaged. That is, they played in games in which even the greediest player could win substantially less than an average player in another treatment condition. There were variations in monetary payoffs for alternative coalitions, in the strength of the utility for equity manipulation, and in the probabilities of being chosen by robot players. In the free-interactive games (reported in Chapter 9) a subject's position could cause a relative disadvantage in his ability to enter coalitions, since the payoff structure favored certain alliances. Therefore, we decided that all subjects should be paid the same amount; two dollars seemed to us to be an equitable payment for less than one hour's work. (When subjects were recruited, they were told that payment would vary depending upon the experiment in which they participated, but that the average payment was approximately two dollars for an hour's time.) When the subjects were told how much they were to be paid and the reasons leading to our decision, they were asked if they felt that this was fair. We offered to pay any individual the amount he actually won if he felt our solution was unsatisfactory. (Only one subject exercised this option.)

6

Ordinal Tests of the Theory

The research discussed in this chapter is concerned with testing the basic assumptions of the theory. The hypotheses are of an ordinal nature. They are concerned with directional changes in variable y as a result of changes in variable x. The following sections will report the test and replication of three predictions of the theory. Each experiment was carried out first on a sample of male subjects and then replicated using a sample of female subjects. Note that the theory does not attempt to predict whether or not males and females will initially assign the same utilities to money and equity. What it does predict is that changes in the parameters of the experiment will have the same, significant effects on both subject populations.

6.1 EXPERIMENT I—THE EFFECTS OF DIFFERENCES IN THE PROBABILITIES OF BEING CHOSEN BY OTHER PLAYERS

The choice theory predicts that the probability of being chosen by another player will directly affect the probability with which an individual chooses that player. In order to test this hypothesis, two conditions were necessary. The control condition, Condition A, was identical to the experimental condition, Condition B, with regard to all factors except the probabilities with which the subject was chosen by the simulated players. Table 6.1 presents a summary of the formal characteristics of the two treatment conditions.

Table 6.1 *Formal Characteristics of Experiment I*

Treatment*	Payoffs for coalitions with players 1 and 2		Probabilities of being chosen by players 1 and 2		Number of trials
	a_1	a_2	π_1	π_2	
Condition A	$.05	$.05	.70	.30	100
Condition B	$.05	$.05	.60	.40	100

*Different groups of subjects were used in each treatment condition (A, B, C, D, etc.) in the research program.

For both conditions, the payoff to the subject for forming either of the possible coalitions was five cents ($a_1 = a_2 = \$.05$). In Condition A the subject was chosen by player one on 70% of the trials ($\pi_1 = .70$) and by player two on 30% of the trials ($\pi_2 = .30$).[1] These percentages were fixed so that in each 10-trial block, the subject was chosen six times only by player one, twice only by player two, once by both and once by neither.

In Condition B, the subject was chosen by player one with a probability of .60 ($\pi_1 = .60$) and by player two with a probability of .40 ($\pi_2 = .40$). In every 10-trial block, he was chosen five times by only player one, three times by only player two, once by both players, and once by neither player. The payoffs for forming coalitions were identical to those used in Condition A ($a_1 = a_2 = \$.05$). There were 100 iterations of the game in each treatment condition. The subjects in both conditions were all males, and all subjects believed that the other players in their game were also male. There were 22 subjects in Condition A and 21 subjects in Condition B.

The only differences between control and experimental conditions were the probabilities with which subjects were chosen by the other players. Theoretically, the effects of the differences between Condition A and Condition B are to diminish the expected utility of a choice of player one and increase the expected utility of a choice of player two. The choice behavior of subjects in

1. For half the subjects, the numbers of the players were reversed. They were chosen by player one with a probability of .30 and player two with a probability of .70. In order to keep the reports of these researches reasonably readable, the robot who chose the subject more frequently will always be identified as player number one.

the two conditions is reported in Table 6.2. The symbols $\bar{P}_1$ and $\bar{P}_2$ refer to the mean probabilities with which subjects select players one and two over the entire series of 100 trials.

Table 6.2 *Probabilities of Coalition Choices in Experiment I*
(Males) *

Treatment	N	Payoff	π_1	π_2	$\bar{P}_1$	$\bar{P}_2$
Condition A	22	$a_1 = a_2 = \$.05$	.70	.30	.8100	.1900
Condition B	21	$a_1 = a_2 = \$.05$	.60	.40	.6162	.3838

*The raw data from all experiments reported in this monograph and the sequence of robot choices used in each treatment condition can be found in Appendix II.

Clearly, the theory correctly predicts the direction of difference in subjects' average choice strategies from Condition A to Condition B.[2] As the probability with which a robot chooses the subject is changed, the probability with which the subject selects that robot is changed. The mean probability with which subjects chose player one, $\bar{P}_1$, was .8100 in Condition A; the corresponding probability in Condition B was .6162. This represents a decrease of .1938 from the control to the experimental condition. (The probability with which subjects chose player two was, of course, affected in the opposite manner.) The probabilities of subject choices vary as a direct function of the probabilities with which they are chosen.

The data from this experiment can be examined from two additional perspectives. The statistical significance of the effects introduced by differences in the experimental conditions, as well as the choice behavior of subjects through time, will be considered.

Figure 6.1 presents a frequency distribution of the mean probability of choosing player one for subjects in the two treatment conditions. Application of a one-tailed Mann-Whitney U Test to this data reveals that the difference between distributions is significant at $P < .001$. The difference in the probability structure of the coalition game significantly affects the choice behavior of players in the game.

In Figure 6.2, process data on the probability of a player one choice are presented for subjects in the two conditions. The choice probabilities are calculated for blocks of 10 trials. Inspection of the data reveals that there is a marked, consistent difference in the behavior of subjects in the two treatment conditions. Subjects in Condition A choose player one with a higher probability throughout the entire experiment.

2. *Strategy* refers to the subject's distribution of choices between the alternative potential coalitions. That is, the probability with which he selects each of the other players.

$\bar{P}_1$	Condition A	Condition B
.96 – 1.	XXX	
.91 – .95	XXX	
.86 – .90	XXXXX	
.81 – .85	X	X
.76 – .80	X	X
.71 – .75	XXXX	XXXXX
.66 – .70	XXX	XXXX
.61 – .65	X	
.56 – .60	X	XXXXX
.51 – .55		
.46 – .50		XXX
≤ .45		XX
	N = 22	N = 21

Figure 6.1 *Mean Player One Choices Per Subject in Experiment I (Males).*

Each facet of the data from this experiment supports the prediction of the theory. Differences in experimental procedures from Condition *A* to Condition *B* produce the expected directional effects; the differences in the subjects' average choice strategies are statistically significant, and the subjects in the two treatment conditions behave differently throughout the experiments.

As the final step in this segment of the research, the experiment was replicated on a small sample of female subjects. The replication serves two purposes. First, it provides a second test of the hypothesis with a different

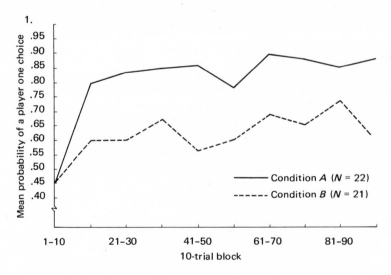

Figure 6.2 *Mean Probability of a Player One Choice Through Time in Experiment I (Males).*

subject population. And, second, by comparing the data from the female sample to those obtained from the males, it is possible to determine whether or not there are any sex-related differences in reactions to this type of social choice situation.[3]

Subjects for the replication were volunteers recruited from the same classes as the males who participated in the first run. There were six subjects in the control condition, Condition A', and nine subjects in the experimental condition, Condition B'. The formal characteristics of the two conditions were identical to those reported in Table 6.1.

Table 6.3 *Probabilities of Coalition Choices in Experiment I (Females)*

Treatment	N	Payoff	π_1	π_2	$\bar{P}_1$	$\bar{P}_2$
Condition A'	6	$a_1 = a_2 = \$.05$	.70	.30	.8433	.1567
Condition B'	9	$a_1 = a_2 = \$.05$	.60	.40	.6889	.3111

Table 6.3 presents the data on the choice strategies adopted by female subjects under the conditions of Experiment I. The data reveal the same general effects as displayed by male subjects under comparable conditions. For the female sample, the effect of decreasing the probability with which player one chooses the subject and increasing the probability of being chosen by player two is to decrease the probability of a player one choice and increase the probability of a player two choice. The magnitude of the effect on the probabilities of these events is .1544.

The same two additional analytical procedures that were performed on the data from the male sample were applied to the data from this sample. The results are essentially identical to those obtained with the male sample. Application of a one-tailed Mann-Whitney U Test to a frequency distribution of the mean probability of a player one choice for subjects in the two conditions (see Figure 6.3) reveals that the probability of these distributions having been obtained from the same population by chance is less than .025. Inspection of the mean probability of a player one choice in 10-trial blocks (see Figure 6.4) indicates that the difference in the experimental setting between Condition A' and Condition B' has a consistent, marked effect on choice behavior.

Experiment I was designed to test the hypothesis that a subject's choice strategy is affected by the probabilities with which he is chosen by the other

---

3. The question of sex differences will not be addressed at this point. This issue is tangential to the major purpose of research being reported here (that is, the development and evaluation of a predictive, utility-based model of decision making) and consideration of sex-related effects, at this time, would unnecessarily complicate the task of reporting the research relevant to the major question.

$\bar{P}_1$	Condition A'	Condition B'
.96 – 1.		
.91 – .95	X	X
.86 – .90	XX	
.81 – .85	X	
.76 – .80	XX	X
.71 – .75		X
.66 – .70		XX
.61 – .65		XX
.56 – .60		XX
⩽ .55		
	N = 6	N = 9

Figure 6.3 *Mean Player One Choices Per Subject in Experiment I (Females).*

players in the game. Theoretically, the experiment tests the effects of changing an independent variable which is assumed to affect the expected utility of a choice, and hence is predicted to affect decision making. In light of the body of evidence generated by the experiment and replication, it is reasonable to conclude that the probability of being chosen affects decision making in the asserted manner.

It is important to note that the differences in the structure of the experiment from Condition *A* to Condition *B* produced effects on both male and female subjects which were not only highly unlikely to have occurred by chance, but were quite substantial and consistent through time. Consider that

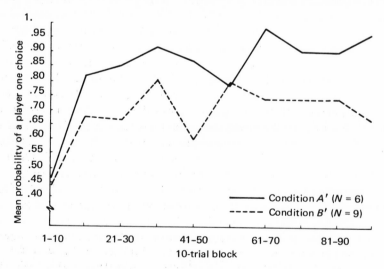

Figure 6.4 *Mean Probability of a Player One Choice Through Time in Experiment I (Females).*

a minimal difference in the probabilities of being chosen by each of the other players (i.e., a .10 decrease in the probability of being chosen by player one and a .10 increase in the probability of being chosen by player two) produces a major shift in the subjects' choice strategies. Males react with a .1938 decrease in the probability of choosing player one, and female subjects evidence a .1544 probability shift. It is clear from inspection of Figures 6.2 and 6.4 that the differences in the structure of the experiment consistently affect subjects. Clearly, the probability of events is causally related to choice behavior. It is equally clear that probabilistic factors have powerful effects on the dependent variable of choice behavior.

6.2 EXPERIMENT II—THE EFFECTS OF DIFFERENCES IN THE PAYOFFS FOR FORMING COALITIONS

The theory predicts that if the payoff for forming a given coalition increases, and all other variables are held constant, the probability of an individual's choosing that coalition increases. The argument leading to this prediction is that as the payoff associated with an alternative increases, the expected utility of that alternative increases, and hence the likelihood of selecting the alternative increases. Theoretically, it is possible to change the expected utility of a choice by changing either the probability of obtaining the payoff associated with the choice or changing the utility of the payoff itself. Experiment I demonstrated that changing the probability of being able to enter a coalition affects an individual's choice strategy. In this experiment, the probability of being chosen by the other players in the game will be held constant, and the payoffs associated with alternatives will be varied.

Two treatment conditions were necessary in order to test the proposed relationship between payoff and choice. The control condition, Condition A, in the previous experiment served as a control condition for this investigation. The experimental condition, Condition C, was made to differ from Condition A in only one respect: the payoffs associated with one of the alternative conditions. The parameters for the two treatment conditions are reported in Table 6.4.

In both conditions, the subject is chosen by player one on 70% of the trials ($\pi_1 = .70$) and by player two on 30% of the trials ($\pi_2 = .30$). The sequence of choices made by the two robot players during the series of 100 trials is identical in the two conditions. In both conditions, the payoff for a coalition with player one is fixed at five cents. The only difference between the two conditions is in the payoff the subject receives for a coalition with player two; in Condition A, the subject receives five cents, and in Condition C he receives 10 cents. The prediction is, of course, that the subjects in Condi-

Table 6.4 *Formal Characteristics of Experiment II*

Treatment	Payoffs for coalitions with players 1 and 2		Probabilities of being chosen by players 1 and 2		Number of trials
	a_1	a_2	π_1	π_2	
Condition A	$.05	$.05	.70	.30	100
Condition C	$.05	$.10	.70	.30	100

tion C will choose player two more frequently than do the subjects in Condition A.

All subjects who participated in the experiment were male and were recruited for the research in the manner previously described. There were 22 subjects in treatment Condition A and 14 subjects in Condition C. Table 6.5 presents the data on the mean probabilities with which subjects chose players one and two ($\bar{P}_1$ and $\bar{P}_2$) over the 100 iterations of the game.

Table 6.5 *Probabilities of Coalition Choices in Experiment II (Males)*

Treatment	N	a_1	a_2	π_1	π_2	$\bar{P}_1$	$\bar{P}_2$
Condition A	22	$.05	$.05	.70	.30	.8100	.1900
Condition C	14	$.05	$.10	.70	.30	.4971	.5029

In Condition A, subjects chose player two with a mean probability of .1900, while in Condition C, subjects chose player two with a mean probability of .5029. The change in the magnitude of payoffs associated with the alternative coalitions between Condition A and Condition C produces an average difference of .3129 in the probability with which subjects choose each of the other players in their game. The effect is in the predicted direction and is quite substantial.

In order to assess the statistical significance of the experimental manipulations and the consistency with which the behavior of subjects is affected, the same procedures used to analyze the data from Experiment I were applied in this case. Figure 6.5 shows the frequency distribution of the mean probabilities with which subjects in each of the treatment conditions choose player one. The difference in the distributions is significant at $P < .001$ with a one-tailed Mann-Whitney U Test.

The process characteristics of the data are presented in Figure 6.6. These graphs show the mean probability of a player one choice in 10-trial blocks for subjects in each of the conditions. The differences in behavior in the two conditions are quite consistent.

$\bar{P}_1$	Condition A	Condition C
.96 – 1.	X X X	
.91 – .95	X X X	
.86 – .90	X X X X X	
.81 – .85	X	
.76 – .80	X	X
.71 – .75	X X X X	X
.66 – .70	X X X	X
.61 – .65	X	
.56 – .60	X	X X X
.51 – .55		X
.46 – .50		X X X
.41 – .45		X
⩽.40		X X X
	N = 22	N = 14

Figure 6.5 *Mean Player One Choices Per Subject in Experiment II (Males).*

As a consistency check on the result reported above, Experiment II was replicated on a small sample of female subjects. The control condition for this experiment was the Condition *A'* treatment reported in connection with Experiment I. The experimental condition, Condition *C'*, is formally identical to the Condition *C* treatment described previously. The characteristics of both treatment conditions are reported in Table 6.4. For the replication, there were

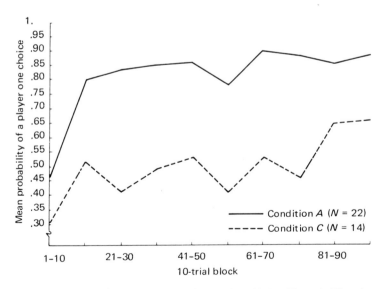

Figure 6.6 *Mean Probability of a Player One Choice Through Time in Experiment II (Males).*

six female subjects in the control condition and eight female subjects in the experimental condition. The results of the replication are summarized in Table 6.6.

Table 6.6 *Probabilities of Coalition Choices in Experiment II (Females)*

Treatment	N	Payoff a_1	a_2	π_1	π_2	$\overline{P}_1$	$\overline{P}_2$
Condition A'	6	$.05	$.05	.70	.30	.8433	.1567
Condition C'	8	$.05	$.10	.70	.30	.4662	.5338

In Condition A, subjects chose player two with a mean probability of .1567, while in Condition C this event occurred with a mean probability of .5338. The effect of increasing the payoff for a coalition with player two was to produce a mean increase of .3771 in the probability with which the subject chose that player. The difference in choice strategy induced through the difference in payoffs for coalitions is pronounced and of the same order of magnitude as observed for the male subjects.

The usual additional analytic procedures were applied to the data with the following results. The Mann-Whitney U Test yields a value which is significant at a probability of less than .001 (one-tailed). Since, as shown in

$\overline{P}_1$	Condition A'	Condition C'
.96 – 1.		
.91 – .95	X	
.86 – .90	XX	
.81 – .85	X	
.76 – .80	XX	
.71 – .75		X
.66 – .70		
.61 – .65		
.56 – .60		
.51 – .55		XX
.46 – .50		
.41 – .45		XXXX
⩽ .40		X
	$N = 6$	$N = 8$

Figure 6.7 *Mean Player One Choices Per Subject in Experiment II (Females).*

Figure 6.7, the distributions of mean probabilities with which subjects in the two conditions choose player one are nonoverlapping, a statement of the significance level is somewhat superfluous.

With regard to the process characteristics of the data, Figure 6.8 reveals that subjects in the two conditions show early and distinct differences in the probabilities with which they choose player one.

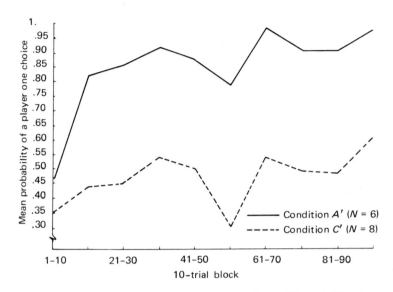

Figure 6.8 *Mean Probability of a Player One Choice Through Time in Experiement II (Females).*

The results of Experiment II and its replication unambiguously support the theory's prediction. For both male and female subjects, the change in the amount of the payoff associated with an alternative has a significant, consistent, and powerful effect on choice strategies.

6.3 EXPERIMENT III—THE EFFECTS OF EQUITY CONSIDERATIONS

In the analysis of the coalition game situation, we argued that it must be recognized that players in this game, and in most social situations, assign utilities to commodities other than money. Up to this point in the research it has been shown that if either of the two factors which are obviously related to the expected value of a choice is experimentally varied, it is possible to produce substantial changes in behavior. At this stage in the experimental program, the problem is to test (1) the viability of the assumption that actors in coalition games assign a positive utility to maintaining an equitable division of the total available rewards among players in the game and (2) the prediction that choice behavior will be affected by changes in the magnitude of utility that actors assign to the maintenance of an equitable division of rewards.

The theory predicts that, if all other variables are held constant, as the utility assigned to the maintenance of equity increases, individuals will tend to distribute their choices of other players more equally. Note that in any coalition game with a fixed probability structure, a player's movement toward a more equal distribution of choices between alternative coalitions results in winning a smaller amount of money. The strategy which results in the greatest monetary win for an individual is to invariably choose the player who chooses him with a higher probability. In effect, the theory argues that as an individual's relative value for maintaining an equitable division of total rewards increases, he will be increasingly likely to attempt to form coalitions with the player who chooses him infrequently. That is, he will behave as if he is giving up some amount of money in order to satisfy his desire to have all the players in the game win more nearly the same total amount of money.

In the context of the coalition game, the magnitude of utility a player assigns to the maintenance of equity is likely to be a function of two factors: the normative definition of the situation and the importance of maintaining good relations with the other players in the game. If, in the description of the game, its aspects of individual gain are stressed, the subject is likely to be relatively unconcerned about the fate of the other players. This low degree of concern will be reinforced if subjects have no particular reason to be concerned with maintaining good relations with the other players (as in the situation in which they do not expect to ever discover which of the other participants were in their particular game). If, on the other hand, the description of the game situation stresses the interdependence of players, subjects are likely to become sensitive to equity considerations. If, in addition, subjects are informed that after the conclusion of the game they will meet with the other players in their particular game to discuss the experience in detail, they would be more likely to be concerned with the quality of the relations that they have with players they are soon to meet in a face-to-face discussion situation.

The preceding paragraph describes the essential differences between the control and experimental conditions for Experiment III. The control condition for this experiment is the Condition *A* previously described. The instructions used in this condition (see Section 5.2) defined the norms in the situation as permitting a player to be concerned solely with maximizing his monetary reward, made it clear that during the experiment it would be impossible to determine with whom he was playing, and gave no reason to suspect that this state of anonymity would ever be changed. The attempt in these instructions was to induce subjects to assign a relatively low utility to equity during the experiment.

The instructions for the experimental condition, Condition *D*, were designed to lead subjects to assign a relatively higher magnitude of utility to maintenance of equity than the level assigned in Condition *A*. This was accomplished by making two changes in the standard form of the instructions.

The first alteration consisted in changing *the last sentence* of the first paragraph. At this point in the low-equity instructions, subjects are told that "Your object [in the game] is to win as much money as you can." In the high-equity manipulation, the last seven sentences of the first paragraph were as follows:

> . . . A game consists of a series of plays; on each play, every participant is asked to choose one of the other players as a coalition partner. If two persons select each other as partners, they have formed a coalition, and each of them receives a reward in the form of money; the third person receives nothing. You can win only by forming a coalition. It is possible that on some plays no one will win. This occurs when no player's choice has been reciprocated. Consequently, on each play, at most two persons can win a reward, and at least one person must lose. *Note that if one player is systematically excluded from coalitions by the other two in his game, he will win almost nothing for today's session.*[4]

The second alteration to the instructions consisted in replacing the last five sentences of the low-equity manipulation with some new material. The first part of the replacement material again stressed the interdependence of players in the game. The added segment informed players that after the conclusion of the game they would meet the other two participants in their particular game. (Note that for the instruction period there were either six or nine individuals in the large room, and no one could be sure with whom he was going to play the coalition game.) The last two paragraphs of the high-equity manipulation were as follows:

> Before you begin playing, let's summarize the main points. You'll be playing a coalition game with two other players. On each play, each of you will choose one of the other two players for a coalition partner. After all of you have made your choices, you will be able to see which of the others has chosen you. If the person whom you have chosen has also chosen you, you will win a monetary reward. *In order to win this reward, you must form coalitions. Note, however, that every time a coalition is formed, one of the three players is excluded. He wins nothing on that trial. It is therefore possible that one player can win almost nothing in this game if neither of the other two players will form coalitions with him. We are interested in studying how three individuals react when they play a coalition game together, when their fates are intertwined so that each one must depend on the others in order to survive. In the game a*

---

4. The change in the text of the instructions is italicized.

player's fate is largely determined by how willing the other two are to allow him into coalitions. If no one will help a player he will do very poorly.

When the game has been completed there will be a discussion period. At this time, each of you will meet with the other two players in his game and discuss what occurred during the play of the game.[5]

Except for the differences in the instructions discussed above, the Condition *A* and Condition *D* treatments were identical. The formal characteristics of the game situation are reported in Table 6.7.

Table 6.7 *Formal Characteristics of Experiment III*

Treatment	Payoffs for coalitions with players 1 and 2		Probabilities of being chosen by players 1 and 2		Equity	Number of trials
	a_1	a_2	$\cdot\pi_1$	π_2		
Condition *A*	$.05	$.05	.70	.30	Low	100
Condition *D*	$.05	$.05	.70	.30	High	100

The subjects in the experiment were all males; there were 22 subjects in the Condition *A* treatment and 11 subjects in Condition *D*. The average probabilities with which subjects in the two conditions chose players one and two are presented in Table 6.8.

Table 6.8 *Probabilities of Coalition Choices in Experiment III (Males)*

Treatment	N	Payoff	π_1	π_2	Equity	$\overline{P}_1$	$\overline{P}_2$
Condition *A*	22	$a_1 = a_2 = \$.05$	.70	.30	Low	.8100	.1900
Condition *D*	11	$a_1 = a_2 = \$.05$	.70	.30	High	.6391	.3609

Subjects in Condition *A* choose player one with a probability of .8100, while subjects in Condition *D* choose player one with a probability of .6391. The difference between the low- and high-equity manipulations produces a difference of .1709 in the average choice strategy of subjects in the two conditions. Note that the direction of the shift in behavior is toward a more equal distribution of choices between the other players in the game.

The distribution of these probabilities over the subjects in the two conditions is shown in Figure 6.9. The difference between distributions is signifi-

5. The changes in the text of the instructions are italicized.

$\overline{P}_1$	Condition A	Condition D
.96 – 1	XXX	
.91 – .95	XXX	
.86 – .90	XXXXX	X
.81 – .85	X	X
.76 – .80	X	
.71 – .75	XXXX	
.66 – .70	XXX	X
.61 – .65	X	XXX
.56 – .60	X	X
.51 – .55		XXX
⩽ .50		X
	N = 22	N = 11

Figure 6.9 *Mean Player One Choices Per Subject in Experiment III (Males).*

cant at $P < .001$ with a one-tailed Mann-Whitney U Test. Figure 6.10 shows the mean probability of a player one choice for each condition by 10-trial blocks. In this experiment, as in the two previous experiments, the effect of the difference in the independent variable is immediate and pronounced throughout the game.

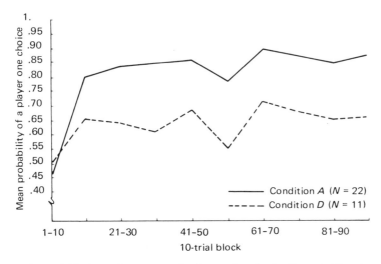

Figure 6.10 *Mean Probability of a Player One Choice Through Time in Experiment III (Males).*

In the replication of the experiment, there were six female subjects in Condition A' and six female subjects in Condition D'. Table 6.9 presents the average probabilities with which the subjects chose each of the other players over the 100 trials.

The average choice strategy adopted by subjects is .2616 closer to a 50-50 distribution in Condition D' than in Condition A'. Figure 6.11 shows the distribution of these probabilities over the subjects in the two conditions. The

Table 6.9 *Probabilities of Coalition Choices in Experiment III (Females)*

Treatment	N	Payoff	π_1	π_2	Equity	$\overline{P}_1$	$\overline{P}_2$
Condition A'	6	$a_1 = a_2 = \$.05$	.70	.30	Low	.8433	.1567
Condition D'	6	$a_1 = a_2 = \$.05$	.70	.30	High	.5817	.4183

difference is significant at $P < .001$ with a one-tailed Mann-Whitney U Test. (The two samples are nonoverlapping.) Figure 6.12 shows the mean probability of a player one choice for each condition in 10-trial blocks. In this case, also, the manipulation shows an early and definite effect.

$\overline{P}_1$	Condition A'	Condition D'
.96 – 1.		
.91 – .95	X	
.86 – .90	XX	
.81 – .85	X	
.76 – .80	XX	
.71 – .75		
.66 – .70		X
.61 – .65		X
.56 – .60		XXX
.51 – .55		
$\leqslant .50$		X
	$N = 6$	$N = 6$

Figure 6.11 *Mean Player One Choices Per Subject in Experiment III (Females).*

Experiment III yields results which are clearly in support of the theory. For both the male and female subjects, the difference in the equity manipulation induces a difference in behavior which is in the predicted direction, is statistically significant, and is strikingly consistent throughout the experiment.

In the analysis of the coalition game situation we argued that a difference in the assignment of a utility for equity could be produced in at least two ways: through a redefinition of the normative structure of the situation or through changing the subject's motivation to maintain good relations with the other players. From the point of view of the choice theory it is irrelevant whether the difference in the utility assignment comes about through a change in one or the other or both of these factors. Given the methodological problem that manipulating a subject's desire for equity is a tricky affair, since it depends on changes in instructions rather than on changes in the more concrete aspects of the structure of the experiment, we decided to change both factors.

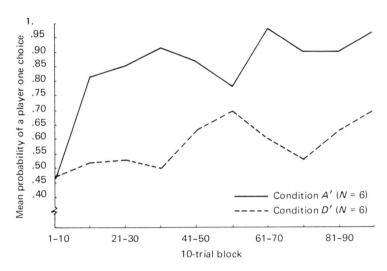

Figure 6.12 *Mean Probability of a Player One Choice Through Time in Experiment III (Females).*

Since the data from Experiment III indicate that there is a considerable effect induced by these joint changes, we decided to create an additional treatment condition in which only one of the equity-affecting factors was manipulated. In this condition, only a change in the normative definition of the situation was manipulated. This was accomplished by changing only those aspects of the standard instructions which stressed maximization of monetary gain and introducing only the statements relating to subject interdependence. No mention was made of subjects meeting for discussions after the conclusion of the game phase of the experiment. In this respect, the instructions were identical to the standard set.

There were nine male subjects in the new treatment condition, Condition *E*. The data generated by subjects run under these instructions are extremely interesting in comparison with Conditions *A* and *D*. The manipulation for this condition was obviously weaker than the one used for Condition *D*, in which a second equity factor was added. The theory, therefore, predicts that the mean probability with which the subjects choose player one in this condition, Condition *E*, will fall between Condition *A* and Condition *D*.

The effects of the three different treatment conditions on choice behavior

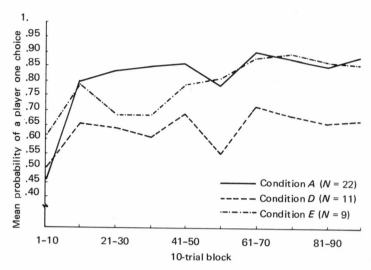

Figure 6.13 *Mean Probability of a Player One Choice Through Time in Experiment III (Males—All).*

are most clearly presented graphically. Figure 6.13 reports the mean probability of a player one choice in 10-trial blocks for each of the treatment conditions. For the first half of the experiment, subjects in Condition E adopt choice strategies roughly intermediate between the strategies adopted by subjects in Conditions A and D. For the last 50 trials, however, it appears that subjects in Conditions A and E adopt identical choice strategies.

$\bar{P}_1$	Condition A	Condition E	Condition D
.96 – 1.	XX	X	
.91 – .95	X		
.86 – .90	XXXX		X
.81 – .85	X		
.76 – .80	XXXXX	XXX	X
.71 – .75	X	X	
.66 – .70	XXX	X	X
.61 – .65	X		X
.56 – .60	XXX	XX	XX
.51 – .55	X		XXXX
.46 – .50			X
.41 – .45		X	
≤ .40			
	$N = 22$	$N = 9$	$N = 11$

Figure 6.14 *Mean Player One Choices Per Subject in the First Half of Experiment III (Males—All).*

Although changing the normative structure of the game situation produces a marked initial effect on behavior, the manipulation is not sufficiently powerful to lead subjects to assign a high utility to maintenance of equity throughout the experiment. In Condition *E*, the mean probability of a player one choice is .7067 for the first half of the experiment and .8600 for the second half. It appears that the equity manipulation decays during the course of the experiment.

If the data from the first and second halves of the experiments are considered separately, the effects of the manipulation and the subsequent decay can be clearly observed. Figures 6.14 and 6.15 report the mean probabilities of player one choices by subjects in Conditions *A*, *E*, and *D* for the first and second halves of the experiments.

$\overline{P}_1$	Condition A	Condition E	Condition D
.96 – 1.	XXXXXXXX	XXX	
.91 – .95	X	X	
.86 – .90	XXXX	XXX	X
.81 – .85	XX		X
.76 – .80	XX		
.71 – .75	XX		XXX
.66 – .70	X		
.61 – .65		XX	
.56 – .60	XX		XXXX
.51 – .55			X
.46 – .50			X
.41 – .45			
≤ .40			
	N = 22	*N* = 9	*N* = 11

Figure 6.15 *Mean Player One Choice Per Subject in the Second Half of Experiment III (Males–All).*

The data from the three experiments are particularly intriguing since they demonstrate that when both the normative structure is changed and an equity manipulation based upon some future event is introduced (Condition *D*), the result is to produce an additive and consistent effect on behavior. That is, combining the two equity factors (as in Condition *D*) produces a greater effect than when only one is present (as in Condition *E*), and their joint effects are sustained throughout the experiment. It seems that linking equity considerations to a future event serves to prevent the decay of the manipulation based solely on a redefinition of the norms of the situation.

Responses to post-session questionnaires and interviews with subjects in Condition *E* support an interpretation that identifies future orientation as an important factor in maintenance of utility for equity. Subjects in this condition reported that they found themselves becoming less and less concerned about the fate of the other players as the experiment progressed. Subjects in Condition *D* reported no such decline in concern. Although the question of the most effective manner in which to alter an individual's assignment of utility for equity in the distribution of rewards is tangential to the main topic of this investigation, it should be noted that the data reported above suggest that future orientation may be a key consideration.

With respect to the major research question, the data from Experiment III clearly support the theory. The introduction of differences in the experimental setting that were designed to increase a subject's utility for equity had the predicted effects for both male and female subjects. The effects of the differences in the parameters of the experiment were statistically significant in every case, and consistent throughout the duration of the experiment for all but one of the treatments. The anomalous data generated in Condition *E* do not introduce any serious doubt as to the appropriateness of the theory's assumption concerning the effects of equity considerations. The data are primarily of interest for what they suggest about boundary conditions on the manipulation of equity.

A Model for Equal
Alpha Conditions

7.1 MEASUREMENT OF UTILITIES

This chapter reports three tests of the predictive power of the choice model under conditions in which the utilities for forming alternative coalitions are equal. Since in the notation of the model the ratio of the utility of a reciprocated choice to the utility for equity is denoted by the symbol α, situations in which the utilities of the payoffs are equal and the utility for equity is fixed are referred to as *equal alpha conditions*.

The structure of the formal model is such that there are three unknowns in the equations used to predict stable-state choice strategies.[1] The unknowns are: (1) the probabilities of being chosen by the other players, (2) the subjects' utility for the payoff for forming a coalition, and (3) the subjects' utility for

---

1. *Stable-state choice strategy* refers to an individual's decision strategy after he has "adjusted" to the situation. In choice experiments of the type discussed in this book, it is typically observed that subjects adopt a stable choice strategy after a learning period of variable length. The model is designed to predict only the subjects' stable-state strategies. It is not intended to account for the "adjustment" or "learning" process prior to stabilization.

equity. Given the values of these three unknowns, the model yields a stable-state choice strategy which maximizes expected utility.

Since the model treats the utilities for equity and for the payoff for forming a coalition rather than the monetary value of the payoff or the strength of the equity-inducing aspects of the experiment, it is necessary to measure the utility of these factors in order to test the model's predictive power. The procedure for testing the model under equal alpha conditions requires a pair of observations, one for measurement and one for testing predictions.

The purpose of the first observation (experiment) is to provide an estimate of the ratio of the utility of the monetary payoff offered for forming a coalition to the utility of equity induced by a specified manipulation. Given all the information from one experiment it is possible to solve the choice equations (derived in Chapter 3) for the ratio of these utilities. That is, the choice equations are structured such that given knowledge of (1) the probabilities with which each of the other players choose the subject and (2) the subject's observed, stable-state choice strategy, it is possible to solve for the ratio of a subject's utility for the monetary payoff (offered for forming a coalition) to his utility for equity. In arriving at this estimate of the subject's utilities, the assumption is made that he acts so as to maximize expected utility in his decision making.

Given the estimate for alpha, it is possible to proceed with a test of the predictive power of the model. Note that up to this point all calculations have been made on the assumption that the model is correct. That is, if subjects act so as to maximize expected utility, and the model correctly formulates the manner in which utilities from different sources are combined, the estimate for alpha will be accurate. In order to *test* the model it is necessary to conduct a second experiment.

In the second, prediction experiment, only one aspect of the situation is changed. Both the equity manipulation and the monetary payoffs for forming coalitions remain the same as in the measurement experiment, while the probabilities with which the subject is chosen by the other players are altered. Theoretically, changing these probabilities has the effect of changing the stable-state strategy which maximizes a subject's expected utility. It has already been shown (Section 6.1) that changing these probabilities affects behavior in the predicted direction. The test of the formal model is its ability to predict the *precise numeric value* of the stable-state strategy adopted by subjects in the second experiment.

Note that the research design calls for estimating alpha with data generated by one group of subjects and using this estimate as a constant in an equation designed to predict the behavior of a second group of subjects in a new situation. In order for the model to predict accurately it must be empirically true that the alpha estimate generated from one sample of subjects can be used to predict behavior for a second population. Although the above statement sounds dangerously like an assertion that the model calls for the assumption that all subjects in the measurement and prediction experiments will assign the same utilities to both equity and a fixed magnitude of money, this is not the case. It is expected that the utilities assigned to these commodities will vary across individuals. The operating assumption employed in the research design is that if individuals are sampled from the same population and randomly assigned to two treatment conditions, subjects in the two samples will assign the same average utilities to payoffs and to maintenance of equity. Although this procedure does not solve the problems which prevent making interpersonal comparisons of utility, it does provide a potentially workable technique for the exploration of utility-based models of human behavior.

The final point to be mentioned in this preface to the report of the evaluation of the equal alpha model concerns the relationship between the measurement and test conditions. It is important to make it quite clear that the measurement condition provides *all of the information* used to generate the predictions for behavior in the test experiment. None of the information used to formulate these predictions is obtained from observations made in the test experiment. Since the observations used for estimation of the parameters are independent of those used to test the model, and the experimental conditions under which measurement and testing are carried out are substantially different, the test is in no sense circular.[2]

7.2 STABILIZATION

The model is designed to predict choice behavior after the subject has reached stable state. It would therefore seem prudent to consider questions pertaining to whether or not subjects in this type of social choice situation attain a stable state and, if so, when it occurs. As was noted earlier (Chapter 4), the length of time it takes to attain stable state is of crucial importance to the generalization of the model to free-interactive behavior. In order to accomplish the generalization it is necessary to assume that individuals tend to make a relatively rapid adjustment to the probabilistic aspects of their social environments. Some evidence suggesting that this may be a viable assumption was reported by Lieberman (1962) and was discussed previously (Chapter 4).

The most straightforward manner in which to explore the issues of

2. Certain of the conditions under which the two sets of data were obtained are held constant. The equity manipulation and the amount of the payoff for forming alternative coalitions are identical in the two conditions. These necessary structural similarities in no way compromise the status of the testing procedure.

stabilization of choice behavior in the coalition game and possible differences between social and nonsocial environments is simply to present graphically data generated in both experimental settings. The data, presented below, on behavior in a two-choice nonsocial setting are typical of results obtained in the Humphreys' light-guessing experiment. This particular set of data was selected because it was obtained in a setting that is formally quite similar to the Condition *A* treatment in the current series of experiments.

The nonsocial choice data were reported by Siegel et al. (1964). It was collected as part of a research program designed to test an application of the general choice model that is being considered here. There were four male subjects in the experiment. The probability with which the more frequent event occurred (illumination of one of a pair of light bulbs) was .75. The less frequent event occurred with a probability of .25. These probabilities were blocked in series of 20 trials. Subjects were paid five cents for every correct prediction.

In Condition *A* of the coalition game experiments there were 22 male subjects. The more frequent event (selection of the subject by player one) occurred with a probability of .70. The less frequent event occurred with a probability of .30. The probabilities were blocked in series of 10 trials. Subjects were paid five cents every time they correctly predicted who was going to choose them.

Although the probabilities of the events that subjects were attempting to predict are not equal in the two experiments, the differences are not sufficiently large to prevent making the necessary comparisons. Figure 7.1 presents the

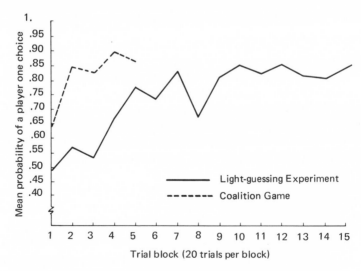

Figure 7.1 *Comparison of Choice Behavior in Social and Nonsocial Situations.*

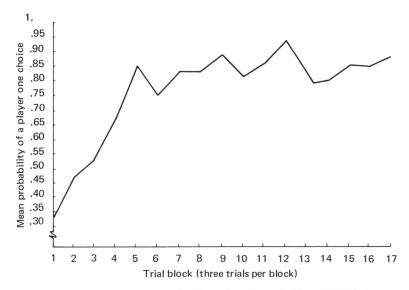

Figure 7.2 *Mean Probability of a Player One Choice in Three-Trial Blocks for Subjects in a Social Situation.*

mean probabilities with which subjects in the two experiments chose the more frequent event.[3] The Siegel experiment was run for 300 trials, while the coalition game was run for only 100 trials.

The differences between the two graphs are striking. In the light-guessing experiment, stabilization occurs after about 200 trials. In the coalition game, subjects appear to stabilize their choice strategies by the end of the first 20-trial block. Subjects in the light-guessing situation move from a .475 initial probability of choosing the more frequently illuminating light to an .850 probability over the course of 200 trials. Subjects in the coalition game shift from a .391 (first five-trial block) probability of choosing player one to a probability of .791 of selecting this player in the third five-trial block. Subjects in the light-guessing experiment evidence a probability shift of .375 over 200 trials. Subjects in the coalition game situation evidence a probability shift of .400 from the first to the third block of five trials. It is obvious that stabilization occurs in the social setting and that it occurs much more rapidly than in the nonsocial choice situation.

In order to obtain a more detailed picture of behavior in the social choice situation, the probability of a choice of the more frequent event was calculated for blocks of three trials for the first half of the experiment (see Figure 7.2). Subjects appear to adjust to the probabilities with which they are

3. The data presented in Figure 7.1 are shown for blocks of 20 trials since this was the block length used in the light-guessing experiment. The authors wish to thank Alberta Engval Siegel for making the data available.

chosen somewhere around the 15th trial. From that point on, their choice behavior can be considered to have stabilized.

It appears reasonable to treat subjects in the social choice situation as attaining a stable-state choice strategy. Further, the data indicate that adaptation to a probability structure is relatively rapid when probabilistic events are believed to be the behaviors of other actors.

7.3 TESTS OF THE EQUAL ALPHA MODEL

Conditions *A* and *B* of the series of experiments already reported (Section 6.1) were designed to permit tests of ordinal predictions of the theory as well as tests of precise numeric predictions derived from the formal model. These two treatment conditions will serve as the measurement and test conditions for the evaluation of the equal alpha model. The two conditions were identical in all respects except for the probabilities with which the robot players chose the subject. Table 7.1 presents a summary of the parameters under which the two experiments were run.

Table 7.1   *Parameters of Experiments Used to Test the Equal Alpha Model*

Treatment	Payoff	π_1	π_2	Equity
Condition *A*	$a_1 = a_2 = \$.05$	.70	.30	Low
Condition *B*	$a_1 = a_2 = \$.05$	.60	.40	Low

The derivation of the equations for the equal alpha model was carried out previously (Chapter 3) and will not be repeated here. The final equations for the model are as follows:

$$P_1 = \frac{\alpha}{4}(\pi_1 - \pi_2) + .5 \qquad P_2 = 1 - P_1$$

where P_x = the probability with which the subject chooses player X,

      π_x = the probability with which the subject is chosen by player X, and

      α = the marginal utility of a reciprocated choice/the marginal utility of equity.

Using all of the information from a measurement experiment, it is possible to obtain values for all but one of the unknowns in the above equations. In these equations, π_1 and π_2 are given conditions set by the experimenter. P_1 (and P_2) are estimated from the observed choice behavior of the subjects after they have reached stabilization. α can be estimated by solving the equation with the given value of π_1 and π_2 and the observed value of P_1.

The alpha estimate obtained from the measurement condition data, together with the values of π_1 and π_2 used in the test experiment, provide all of the information necessary to derive predictions for P_1 and P_2 under test conditions. Note that the values of π_1 and π_2 are different in the two experiments. In Condition A these values are .70 and .30, while in Condition B they are .60 and .40. The predicted values of P_1 and P_2 in the test condition will be different from what they were in the measurement condition.

It is obvious that either of the two treatment conditions could be selected as the measurement experiment with the other serving as the test experiment. That is, it is permissible to use either Condition A to predict behavior in Condition B, or the reverse. Consequently, the model will be tested in both directions. These are, of course, not independent tests, but rather one test simply carried out in two directions as a consistency check.

Since the model requires that subjects be in stable state when its predictions are applied, it is necessary to select some point in the experiment beyond which subjects are considered to have stabilized their choice behavior. There are no analytic procedures which permit identification of this transition point. We therefore decided to apply the model using two different estimates of stable-state behavior. The first estimate is based on calculation of the subjects' choice strategies in the last 20 trials of the experiment. This was the procedure usually followed by Siegel in his work with the choice model. The second procedure is based on selection of the apparent point of stabilization through inspection of the data.

Unfortunately, both procedures are less than ideal solutions to the selection issue. Despite the fact that the former has precedent in its favor, the latter would appear to make somewhat more sense given the aims of the model. For at least these first tests of the model, both methods will be employed.

7.4 PREDICTIONS BASED ON THE LAST TWENTY TRIALS OF THE EXPERIMENTS

The model will first be applied to data generated by male subjects in the Condition A and B treatments. The mean probabilities with which subjects chose players one and two in the last 20 trials in the two conditions are shown in Table 7.2.

Table 7.2 *Mean Stable-State Probabilities of Choices of Players One and Two (Males)*

Treatment	N	$\bar{P}_1$	$\bar{P}_2$
Condition A	22	.8636	.1364
Condition B	21	.6810	.3190

If Condition *A* is used as the measurement experiment, the following value of alpha is obtained:

$$\alpha = (P_1 - .5)\left(\frac{4}{\pi_1 - \pi_2}\right)$$

$$= (.863636 - .5)\left(\frac{4}{.7 - .3}\right)$$

$$= 3.63636$$

This alpha value can be used in the equation in order to predict choice strategies in Condition *B*. The predictions for P_1 and P_2 in Condition *B* are as follows:

$$P_1 = \frac{\alpha}{4}(\pi_1 - \pi_2) + .5$$

$$= \frac{3.63636}{4}(.6 - .4) + .5$$

$$= .6818 \qquad P_2 = 1 - P_1 = .3182$$

The observed values for P_1 and P_2 in Condition *B* were: $\overline{P}_1 = .6810$ and $\overline{P}_2 = .3190$. The absolute value of the discrepancies between the observed and predicted values was .0008 for both P_1 and P_2.

If Condition *B* is used as the measurement experiment, alpha takes the following value:

$$\alpha = (P_1 - .5)\left(\frac{4}{\pi_1 - \pi_2}\right)$$

$$= (.680952 - .5)\left(\frac{4}{.6 - .4}\right)$$

$$= 3.61905$$

Given this estimate for alpha, a prediction can be generated for the stable-state choice strategy of subjects in Condition *A*.

$$P_1 = \frac{\alpha}{4}(\pi_1 - \pi_2) + .5$$

$$= \frac{3.61905}{4}(.7 - .3) + .5$$

$$= .8619 \qquad P_2 = 1 - P_1 = .1381$$

In this case, the absolute value of the discrepancies between the predicted and observed choice strategies was .0017: predicted $P_1 = .8619$; observed

$\overline{P}_1 = .8636$; for P_2 the predicted and observed strategies were .1381 and .1364.

Table 7.3 summarizes the results of these two applications of the model.

Table 7.3 *Results of Application of the Equal Alpha Model (Males)*

Measurement experiment	Prediction experiment	Alpha estimate	Predicted P_1 and P_2	Observed P_1 and P_2	|Discrepancy|
			.6818	.6810	
Condition A	Condition B	3.63636			.0008
			.3182	.3190	
			.8619	.8636	
Condition B	Condition A	3.61905			.0017
			.1381	.1364	

Note that the difference in subjects' choice strategies from one condition to the other is substantial (on the order of 18 points). The model accurately predicts the new choice strategy induced by using a different set of probabilities to determine the frequencies with which the subject was chosen by the other players.

A second, independent test of the model's predictive power can be carried out using the data provided by the two small samples of female subjects run in Conditions *A* and *B* of the experiments. There were six subjects in the Condition *A'* treatment and nine subjects in the Condition *B'* treatment. Although the sample sizes are extremely small for the type of prediction the model is designed to make, it is worthwhile to proceed with the test in order to explore the power of the model under adverse conditions.

Table 7.4 *Mean Stable-State Probabilities of Choices of Players One and Two (Females)*

Treatment	N	$\overline{P}_1$	$\overline{P}_2$
Condition A'	6	.9333	.0667
Condition B'	9	.7056	.2944

Table 7.4 presents the mean probabilities with which the female subjects chose players one and two in the last 20 trials in each of the experiments.

The procedure of first estimating alpha from the data generated in Condition *A'* in order to predict behavior of subjects in Condition *B'*, and then reversing the direction of the procedure (using *B'* for measurement and predicting *A'*), was repeated with the data obtained from the female subjects.

It is unnecessary to reproduce the step-by-step solution for the alpha value in the measurement condition and the subsequent derivation of a prediction for behavior in the test condition. The equations are straightforward, and all of the information necessary to reproduce the solutions for the alpha and P values are presented in Table 7.4. The results of the new application of the model are presented in Table 7.5.

Table 7.5   *Results of Application of the Equal Alpha Model (Females)*

Measurement experiment	Prediction experiment	Alpha estimate	Predicted P_1 and P_2	Observed P_1 and P_2	|Discrepancy|
Condition A'	Condition B'	4.33333	.7167	.7056	.0111
			.2833	.2944	
Condition B'	Condition A'	4.11112	.9111	.9333	.0222
			.0889	.0667	

Using A' for measurement and predicting to B', the model yields a value which is .0111 discrepant from the observed choice strategy of subjects in Condition B'. Going in the other direction, the discrepancy between predicted and observed strategies is .0222. Although the accuracy of the model's predictions is somewhat less than that obtained with the male subjects, the results are quite respectable. Consider that the number of subjects in the two samples was small (six in Condition A' and nine in Condition B'), the difference between the maximizing choice strategies in the two experiments was substantial (a probability difference of about 15 points), and the predicted strategies differ from those observed by very little (.01 and .02).

7.5 PREDICTIONS BASED ON SELECTION OF A STABILIZATION POINT BY INSPECTION

Considering that subjects demonstrate a great sensitivity to probabilistic aspects of the experimental situation, it is reasonable to identify empirically the point of stabilization rather than simply rely on the assumption that if stabilization occurs, it will have done so by the last 20 trials of the experiment. Identification of the earliest reasonable stabilization point offers a substantial advantage over the alternative procedure in that it is likely to permit utilization of more data than is provided in the final 20 trials of each experiment.

Since, as shown earlier, subjects are highly sensitive and adjust rapidly to the sequence of choices made by the robot players, there is more variation in behavior in the coalition game situation than is typically observed in light-guessing experiments. That is, the combination of events, the sequence of player one and two choices, has a powerful effect on behavior in any trial block. Consider the following hypothetical case. If, in a given block, player one chose the subject on seven consecutive trials and then rejected him on the remaining three, it might have happened by the sixth or seventh choice that the subject came to believe that he had entered a stable alliance with player one. Player one's failure to continue the alliance on the seventh trial could lead to anger on the part of the subject. This, in turn, could lead the subject to behave in a rather aberrant fashion for the following few trials. Given that subjects impute a "meaning" to the acts of the robots, it is not surprising to find considerable variability introduced by sequences of choices.

Increasing the number of trials on which measurements and predictions are based has the additional effect of increasing the number of different robot player choice sequences employed during the period of observation. The net result is therefore to increase the number of observations on which predictions are based as well as to partially control the effects of unique sequences of robot player behaviors. These two gains are particularly important when sample sizes are small and the experiments are complex. Although the prediction task in the equal alpha experiments is relatively simple, situations to which the model will be applied in future researches are substantially more complex, and hence safeguards against unanticipated effects are relatively more important.

Inspection of the data generated by male subjects in the Condition *A* and *B* treatments leads to selection of the second and seventh blocks as the starting points for estimates of the values of stable-state choice strategies. (Graphs reporting this data can be found in Chapter 6.) Given these two

Table 7.6 *Mean Probabilities of Choice Strategies with Stabilization Based on Inspection (Males)*

Treatment	N	$\bar{P}_1$	$\bar{P}_2$
Condition A	22	.8495	.1505
Condition B	21	.6750	.3250

starting points, the last 90 trials of the Condition *A* experiment and the last 40 trials of the Condition *B* treatment provide data for testing the model.[4] The mean choice strategies adopted by subjects in the two conditions are presented in Table 7.6.

4. A consistent result in all of the present research is that the greater the difference from a .5 probability of being chosen by each of the other players, the more rapidly do subjects attain stable state.

As expected, application of the model to this data yields results that are somewhat better than those obtained when estimates are based on only the last 20 trials. The results are reported in Table 7.7. The discrepancies obtained

Table 7.7 *Application of the Equal Alpha Model with Stabilization Based on Inspection (Males)*

Measurement experiment	Prediction experiment	Alpha estimate	Predicted P_1 and P_2	Observed P_1 and P_2	|Discrepancy|
			.6747	.6750	
Condition A	Condition B	3.49495			.0003
			.3253	.3250	
			.8500	.8495	
Condition B	Condition A	3.50000			.0005
			.1500	.1505	

with the first application of the model were .0008 using *A* as the measurement experiment and .0017 when *B* was used for measurement. The discrepancies in the present application were .0003 and .0005 using first *A* and then *B* as the measurement experiments. The significance of these results is twofold: (1) they show the model to work better when the amount of data used for observation is increased, and (2) they provide an additional demonstration of the model's considerable predictive power. The latter factor serves to raise subjective confidence in the theory, even if the conditions of this application differ only minimally from those already reported.

For the female subjects, estimates of the earliest reasonable stabilization point are the seventh block for subjects in both experiments. Inspection of the process data from these experiments (Chapter 6) indicates that the female subjects in Condition *A'* take longer to stabilize their choice strategies than do male subjects in comparable circumstances. The mean probabilities for choices over the last 40 trials for subjects in the two treatment conditions are presented in Table 7.8.

Table 7.8 *Mean Probabilities of Choice Strategies with Stabilization Based on Inspection (Females)*

Treatment	N	$\bar{P}_1$	$\bar{P}_2$
Condition A'	6	.9375	.0625
Condition B'	9	.7250	.2750

Increasing the number of observations used in obtaining measurements and predicting to a larger segment of behavior has a more substantial effect on the predictions for the female sample. This is not surprising since the sample sizes for these experiments were quite small. The results of the two applications of the model are presented in Table 7.9.

Table 7.9 *Application of the Equal Alpha Model with Stabilization Based on Inspection (Females)*

Measurement experiment	Prediction experiment	Alpha estimate	Predicted P_1 and P_2	Observed P_1 and P_2	|Discrepancy|
			.7188	.7250	
Condition A'	Condition B'	4.37500			.0062
			.2812	.2750	
			.9500	.9375	
Condition B'	Condition A'	4.50000			.0125
			.0500	.0625	

The absolute value of the discrepancies obtained with the larger segments of behavior compare favorably with those obtained using only the last 20 trials of the experiments. In the earlier applications, the discrepancies between predicted and observed behaviors were .0111 and .0222 using first A' and then B' as the measurement experiment. In this case, the comparable discrepancies were .0062 and .0125.

Comparison of results obtained with the two estimation procedures would suggest that the latter, basing a decision on inspection of behavior, is preferable to the more arbitrary procedure of selection of the last 20 trials of the experiment. The increased predictive power of the model is not as important a consideration as the fact that using larger segments of behavior for measurement and prediction provides a safeguard against unanticipated effects introduced by the fixed sequence of choices made by the robot players. For future applications of the model, the latter procedure will be employed in selection of stabilization points.

7.6 MEASUREMENT AND PREDICTION WITH ONE SAMPLE OF SUBJECTS

Up to this point, all of the applications of the model have been carried out with one sample of subjects supplying data for estimation and a second set being employed in the prediction experiment. The model can, however, be tested with the same sample of subjects, or single subject, supplying both the data with which to estimate alpha and the data against which predictions are compared. That is, it can be applied to an experiment in which subjects serve as their own controls. In some respects, this is a more straightforward, but also less severe, testing procedure than one which calls for using different sets of subjects in the measurement and prediction experiments. The latter procedure requires the assumption to be made that if subjects are sampled from a single population and randomly assigned to treatment conditions, the distributions of utilities for the monetary payoffs and for equity will be identical for subjects in each treatment condition. Since the model accurately predicts choice strategies with this test procedure, it must be the case that the operating assumption concerning equivalence of average utility assignments for successive samples from the same population is tenable. In general, an accurate prediction under this test condition is more impressive than an equally precise prediction made with the simpler testing procedure.

One important point which is not addressed by research carried out with the procedure utilized in all previous applications of the model concerns the stability of utility assignments by subjects faced with two or more different experimental treatments. It has been demonstrated that it is possible to use utility estimates obtained with one set of subjects in order to predict the behavior of a second set of individuals, but it has not been shown that the same subject can be treated as having stable utility assignments when faced with varying environments. The experiment reported in this section was designed to test the viability of this assumption.

The research designed to investigate this question employed a single sample of eight male subjects who participated in a coalition game in which they were chosen by two robot players. The robots were operated with different parameters for the first and second 50 iterations of the game. From the subject's viewpoint, the series of 100 repetitions of the game was continuous. There was no break of any sort at trial 50. In this respect, Experiment IV was identical to all previous experiments. At trial 50, the robots simply changed their choice strategies.

The data from the first half of the experiment were used in order to estimate alpha both for the *group* of subjects and for *each* subject separately. The group alpha estimate was then used to predict the average choice strategy

Table 7.10 *Formal Characteristics of Experiment IV*

Treatment	Payoffs for coalitions with players 1 and 2	Probabilities of being chosen by players 1 and 2	
		Trials 1-50	Trials 51-100
Condition F	$a_1 = \$.05$	$\pi_1 = .70$	.30
	$a_2 = \$.05$	$\pi_2 = .30$	.70

of the group of subjects in the second half of the game. The individual alpha estimates were used to *predict the particular choice strategy each subject should adopt* in the second half of the experiment if he were acting so as to maximize expected utility in his decision making. The formal characteristics of the experiment are summarized in Table 7.10.

The change in the parameters with which the subjects were chosen by the robots had a marked effect on the choice strategies adopted in the first and the second halves of the experiment. Table 7.11 presents the data on the

Table 7.11 *Probabilities of Coalition Choices in Experiment IV*

Treatment	N	Trials 11-50	Trials 61-100
Condition *F*	8	$\bar{P}_1 = .8250$	$\bar{P}_1 = .1969$
		$\bar{P}_2 = .1750$	$\bar{P}_2 = .8031$

mean stable-state probability with which subjects chose each of the robots for the different sets of parameters with which the robots chose the subject.[5] During the first half of the experiment the probability with which a subject was chosen by player one was .70, and the probability with which the subject chose player one was .8250. During the second half of the experiment, the subject was chosen by player one with a probability of .30 and responded with a probability of a player one choice of .1969. From the first to the second half of the experiment, subjects demonstrated a shift in choice strategy of .6281.

It was shown earlier in this chapter that subjects adapt to the probability structure of perceived social situations with greater speed than they exhibit in nonsocial environments. The data obtained in this experiment permit analysis of the effects of prior adjustment to a probability structure on sensitivity to changes in its parameters. The appropriate expectation for the subjects' relative sensitivity to a new probability structure introduced after 50 trials is unclear. That is, should subjects be expected to react with greater or less sensitivity than was shown to the structure operating at the outset of the experiment? It could be argued that if subjects "learn" the probability structure, they would have to go through a period of extinction prior to "learning" the new probabilities, and hence it should take relatively longer to stabilize choice strategies after the mid-game shift than at the start of the game when there was no existing strategy to be extinguished. If, however, subjects are thought of as adapting to the probabilistic aspects of

5. The stable-state choice strategies reported in Table 7.11 are calculated from the data on the last 40 trials in each half of the experiment (i.e., trials 11–50 and 61–100).

their environments, their adaption to the changed parameters of the experiment ought to be at least as rapid as it was at the start of the game. Data on the mean probability of a player one choice through time are presented in Figure 7.3.

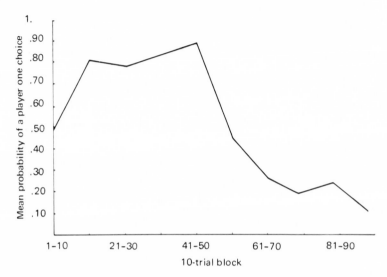

Figure 7.3 *Mean Probability of a Player One Choice Through Time in Experiment IV.*

Note that initially subjects in Experiment IV demonstrate the same rapid adjustment to the behavior of the simulated players as did subjects in Experiment I (see Figure 7.2). For the first 50 trials, Experiment I is identical to Experiment IV. Subjects in Experiment IV appear to stabilize their choice strategies after approximately 10 iterations of the game. Following the reversal of parameters at trial 50, subjects move to their new choice strategies with about the same speed as they showed in their original adjustment to the environment. They reach their new stable-state choice strategies after about 10 iterations of the game.

Since data were obtained from a single group of subjects under equal alpha conditions and with two different sets of π values, it is possible to estimate the ratio of the marginal utility of the monetary payoff for forming a coalition to the marginal utility for equity for both the group as a whole and for each group member separately. The model will first be applied to the data from the group as a whole. Given the mean stable-state probabilities of player one and two choices (reported in Table 7.11) and the choice equations presented at the outset of this book (see Chapter 4), predictions can be derived for the maximizing choice strategy under the changed values of π_1 and π_2. Table 7.12 presents the results of this application of the model.

Table 7.12 *Results of Application of the Equal Alpha Model to Data from a Single Sample of Subjects*

Measurement condition	Prediction condition	Alpha estimate	Predicted P_1 and P_2	Observed P_1 and P_2	|Discrepancy|
			.1750	.1969	
Trials 11-50	Trials 61-100	3.25000			.0219
			.8250	.8031	

Using the data from trials 11 through 50 as the basis on which to estimate alpha, the result is a value of 3.25000. The model therefore yields a prediction for the maximizing choice strategy of $P_1 = .1750$ and $P_2 = .8250$ under the changed probability structure of the second half of the experiment. The observed choice strategy for the second half of the experiment was $P_1 = .1969$ and $P_2 = .8031$. The absolute value of the discrepancy between the observed and predicted strategies was .0219. (This result is equivalent to the one obtained with the similarly small samples of female subjects previously reported.) Clearly, the utility estimates obtained from a set of subjects under one set of environmental conditions can be employed to predict their behavior under a changed set of conditions. The evidence indicates that subjects can be regarded as having stable utility assignments under the two sets of experimental conditions.

The conditions under which Experiment IV were conducted permit an investigation of the power of the model to measure each subject's unique utility assignment and to predict his behavior under the changed parameters of the second half of the experiment. Table 7.13 presents, for 10-trial blocks, the number of player one choices made by each subject throughout the course of the experiment. Note that blocks one and six are transition periods during

Table 7.13 *Number of Player One Choices Under Two Probability Structures*

	Measurement condition					Prediction condition				
	Block number*					Block number				
Subject	1	2	3	4	5	6	7	8	9	10
1	5	7	6	8	6	1	3	6	5	2
2	2	10	10	10	10	10	1	0	0	0
3	4	9	7	6	10	4	0	0	3	2
4	5	8	6	5	9	0	4	3	5	3
5	6	8	10	10	10	9	10	3	0	0
6	7	7	4	8	6	5	3	3	5	2
7	5	9	10	10	10	4	0	0	0	0
8	5	7	9	9	10	3	0	0	0	0

*Blocks are for series of 10 trials.

which time subjects adapt to the two different probability structures employed in the experiment. Blocks two to five and seven to 10 provide the data used for conducting measurements and testing predictions.

In attempting to apply the model to the behavior of single individuals, the data for measurement come from his 40, stable-state decisions made from trial 11 to trial 50 of the experiment. The model's predictions are evaluated against the subject's observed behavior during the last 40 trials of the experiment. In the first half of the experiment, subjects were chosen by player one with a probability of .70 and by player two with a probability of .30. In the second half, they were chosen by player one with a probability of .30 and by player two with a probability of .70.

Since the model attempts to predict the decision behavior of a subject on only 40 trials, it makes little sense to express its predictions in terms of probabilities of player one and two choices. Instead, the predictions will be made in terms of the *number* of player one and two choices over the 40 trials that a subject would make if he were acting so as to maximize expected utility in his decision making and if the model correctly estimates the ratio of his marginal utility for the monetary payoff for forming a coalition to his marginal utility for equity. Table 7.14 summarizes the results of the eight separate applications of the model.

Of the eight applications of the model, only one yields a prediction which is substantially discrepant from the subject's actual choice behavior. This is the prediction for subject number five. In this case, the model predicts that the subject should choose player one only twice during the second half of the experiment and he chooses the player one alternative on 13 of the 40 trials. If the data in Table 7.13 are inspected, it can clearly be seen that subject five takes longer than the usual 10 trials to adapt to the changed probability structure and stabilize his choice strategy. Note that he is the only subject who continues to select player one with great frequency in the seventh trial block. If the reasonable assumption is made that subject five does not stabilize his choice strategy until the eighth trial block and the model is then reapplied, its prediction is that he will make only $1\frac{1}{2}$ choices of player one and $38\frac{1}{2}$ choices of player two. Subject five's observed choice strategy is to make three choices of player one and 37 choices for player two. With the new stabilization point, the absolute discrepancy between his observed and predicted choice strategy is only $1\frac{1}{2}$ choices.

The model accurately predicts the choice strategies adopted by individual subjects when their utilities for the ratio of the monetary reward for forming a coalition to the utility for equity are estimated from their behavior on 40 iterations of the coalition game under one set of experimental conditions and predictions are tested against behavior under a different set of experimental conditions. Although the amount of data used to estimate a single individual's utilities is quite small, and despite the fact that experimental

Table 7.14 *Application of the Equal Alpha Model to the Behavior of Single Individuals*

Subject	Alpha estimate	Predicted number of choices of players 1 and 2	Observed number of choices of players 1 and 2	|Discrepancy|
1	1.67500	P_1 = 13	16	3
		P_2 = 27	24	
2	5.00000	P_1 = 0	1	1
		P_2 = 40	39	
3	2.50000	P_1 = 8	5	3
		P_2 = 32	35	
4	3.00000	P_1 = 12	15	3
		P_2 = 28	25	
5	4.50000	P_1 = 2	13	11
		P_2 = 38	27	
6	1.65000	P_1 = 15	13	2
		P_2 = 25	27	
7	4.97500	P_1 = 1	0	1
		P_2 = 39	40	
8	3.75000	P_1 = 5	0	5
		P_2 = 35	40	

conditions under which predictions were tested were substantially changed from what they were when alpha was estimated, the model generates satisfactory predictions. The range of the discrepancies between the predicted and observed choice strategies is from one to five choices.

7.7 SUMMARY

The equal alpha version of the formal choice model was subjected to two independent tests with estimates for the alpha values generated in two different fashions. For both independent tests, and with both estimation procedures, the model yields predictions for choice behavior which are exceedingly accurate. In a third test, alpha estimates were obtained from data generated by subjects under one set of conditions and then used to predict the behavior of the same subjects under different experimental conditions.

The only appropriate comparisons for the results of these applications of the model are with the results of its first tests in a nonsocial choice situation. In these researches (Siegel et al., 1964), the equal alpha version of the model was tested on three sets of data. Absolute discrepancies between the observed and predicted values of the choice strategies went from a low of .005 to a high of .020. It is surprising that in the social choice situation, with its inherently greater noise, the model should prove equally powerful. In the applications of the model reported here, the discrepancies between observed and predicted strategies ran from a low of .0003 to a high of .0222.

$$8$$

A Model for Unequal
Alpha Conditions

8.1 BASIC EXPERIMENTAL TESTS

This chapter reports a test of the predictive power of the unequal alpha version of the choice model. The unequal alpha model is appropriate for situations in which the ratio of the marginal utility for forming a coalition to the marginal utility for equity is different for an individual's two possible coalitions. We first consider the characteristics and results of three investigations which were conducted in order to obtain sufficient data to test the model. The remainder of this chapter then deals with the three applications of the model that can be made with these data.

The data with which the unequal alpha form of the model was tested were generated in three treatment conditions. In each of these treatments, the subject was confronted with a situation in which he could obtain five cents each time he formed a coalition with player number one and 10 cents for a coalition with player number two. The equity-inducing aspects of the experiments were held constant by using the same set of instructions in all three conditions. (The instructions are reported in Section 5.2.) Since alpha defines the ratio of an individual's utility for the payoff associated with a coalition to his utility for equity, and the utilities of the payoffs are different for the two alternative coalitions while the utility for equity is a constant in the experiment, the alpha values for alternative coalitions are unequal. The value of alpha for a coalition with player two (the 10-cent alternative) is greater than the value of alpha for a coalition with player one (the five-cent alternative).

The only variables which were changed between experimental conditions were the values of the π parameters. In Condition G the subject was chosen by player one with a probability of .80 and by player two with a probability of .20. In Condition C the corresponding values were .70 and .30. In Condition H these values were .60 and .40. Only male subjects participated in the set of researches (Experiment V). The formal characteristics of the three treatment conditions are summarized in Table 8.1.

Table 8.1 *Formal Characteristics of Experiment V*

Treatment	Payoffs for coalitions with players 1 and 2		Probabilities of being chosen by players 1 and 2		Number of trials
	a_1	a_2	π_1	π_2	
Condition G	$.05	$.10	.80	.20	100
Condition C	$.05	$.10	.70	.30	100
Condition H	$.05	$.10	.60	.40	100

Since the only variables that were changed between treatment conditions were the values of the π parameters, derivation of the theory's ordinal prediction is quite straightforward. Note that the probability of being chosen by player one decreases from Condition G to Condition C, and the probability of being chosen by player two is simultaneously increased. Since expected utility is a product of the utility of a payoff and the probability with which it is obtained, it follows that the expected utility of a player one choice decreases from G to C and the expected utility of a player two choice increases. For the same reasons, it is clear that under the π value of Condition H, the expected utility of a player one choice is lower than it is in Condition C. The theory therefore predicts that the mean probability of a player one choice should decrease from Condition G to Condition C and from Condition C to Condition H ($\bar{P}_1 G > \bar{P}_1 C > \bar{P}_1 H$). The mean probabilities of player one and two choices for subjects in each of the treatment conditions are reported in Table 8.2.

The effects of the differences in experimental treatments are as predicted by the theory. As the probability of being chosen by player one decreases and the probability of being chosen by player two increases, subjects change their

Table 8.2 *Mean Probabilities of Coalition Choices in Experiment V*

Treatment	N	a_1	a_2	π_1	π_2	$\bar{P}_1$	$\bar{P}_2$
Condition G	9	$.05	$.10	.80	.20	.6478	.3522
Condition C	14	$.05	$.10	.70	.30	.4971	.5029
Condition H	13	$.05	$.10	.60	.40	.4323	.5677

behavior in the manner that would be expected if they were acting so as to maximize expected utility. The mean probability of choosing player one decreases from .6478 to .4971 to .4323 from Conditions G to C to H.

Figure 8.1 presents frequency distributions of the mean probabilities of choosing player one for each subject in the three experimental treatments. Since there are three samples and the theory predicts an order for mean probability values, the Jonckheere k-sample Test against ordered alternatives (Jonckheere, 1954) is an appropriate analytic device. This test permits testing of the null hypothesis of no difference between samples against the alternative that the k-samples are drawn from k different populations whose mean values are stochastically ordered in a specified fashion. The prediction to be tested against the hypothesis of no difference is that the three samples were drawn

$\bar{P}_1$	Condition G	Condition C	Condition H
.96 – 1.	X		
.91 – .95			
.86 – .90			
.81 – .85			
.76 – .80	XX	X	
.71 – .75	X	X	
.66 – .70		X	
.61 – .65			
.56 – .60	XX	XXX	XX
.51 – .55	XX	X	XX
.46 – .50		XXX	XX
.41 – .45		X	XX
.36 – .40			XXX
.31 – .35		X	X
.26 – .30	X	X	
.21 – .25			
.16 – .20			
.11 – .15			
.06 – .10			X
0 – .05		X	
	$N = 9$	$N = 14$	$N = 13$

Figure 8.1 *Mean Player One Choices Per Subject in Experiment V.*

from three different populations whose mean values of the probability of a player one choice are ordered $G > C > H$. The test reveals that the probability that the three samples were drawn from the same population is less than .001. The preferred alternative is that the three samples were drawn from three populations that are ordered as specified above.

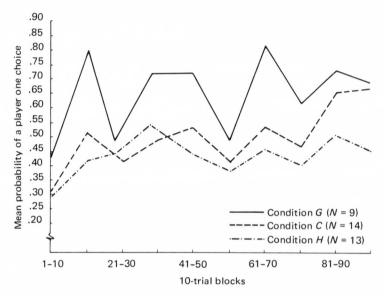

Figure 8.2 *Mean Probability of a Player One Choice Through Time in Experiment V.*

Figure 8.2 presents the process data on the probability of a player one choice for subjects in the three conditions. The probabilities are calculated for blocks of 10 trials. Inspection of the data reveals that after an initial period of adaptation there is a consistent effect introduced by the differences in treatment conditions. As in the process data presented previously, the behavior of subjects in different treatment conditions consistently varies as a function of the characteristics of the experiment in which they participated.

Experiment V provides the data necessary to test the power of the unequal alpha model and also serves as a second, independent test of the postulated relationship between the probability of being able to enter a coalition and an individual's choice behavior. The argument of the theory is that expected utility varies as a function of both the utility of a payoff and the probability with which it is obtained, and individuals act so as to maximize expected utility in their decision making. Therefore, if either expected utility-determining variable (payoff or probability of being chosen) is held constant while the other is varied, the effect is to change the individual's maximizing choice strategy. In Experiment I (Chapter 6), the payoffs for forming alternative coalitions were held constant, while the probabilities of being chosen by the other players were varied. The result was to produce shifts in choice behavior in the direction predicted by the theory. In Experiment I, the payoffs for forming alternative coalitions were equal: $a_1 = a_2 = \$.05$. Experiment V tests the same prediction of the theory under a different set of concrete conditions. In this case the subject is faced with a situation in which the payoff for a coalition with player one is five cents and the payoff for a coalition with player two is 10 cents ($a_1 = \$.05$, $a_2 = \$.10$). The payoff variable is held constant in the three treatment conditions, and the probabilities of being chosen by the other players are varied across conditions. Since in this experiment subjects have a clear preference for forming coalitions with player two, Experiment V poses a more complex decision problem than that faced by subjects in Experiment I. The results of Experiment V indicate that the increased complexity of the decision problem in no way affects the power of the theory to generate correct ordinal predictions for choice behavior.

8.2 STABILIZATION OF CHOICE STRATEGIES UNDER UNEQUAL ALPHA CONDITIONS

The final step prior to conducting a test of the unequal alpha form of the model is to identify that segment of each treatment condition within which subjects will be considered to have stabilized their choice strategies.

In selecting the stabilization points the same procedure was followed as was employed by Siegel in his research with the light-guessing experiment. Under the more complex conditions of unequal alpha experiments, Siegel "decided in advance that the set of trial blocks to be used in estimating the stable state would not be identified until the data were collected and examined" (Siegel et al., 1964, p. 125). When the data reported in Figure 8.2 are considered, the segments of the experiments in which stable-state choice strategies are in evidence appear to be the last 90 trials of Condition *G* and the last 60 trials of Conditions *C* and *H*. That is, trials 11 through 100 in Condition *G* and trials 41 through 100 in the remaining two treatment conditions.

Given the stabilization points identified above, the mean values of the stable-state choice strategies adopted by subjects in the three treatment conditions are as reported in Table 8.3. The differences between the average stable-state choice strategies adopted by subjects in the three conditions are

Table 8.3 *Mean Stable-State Probabilities*
of Player One and Two Choices
in Experiment V

Treatment	N	$\bar{P}_1$	$\bar{P}_2$
Condition G	9	.6716	.3284
Condition C	14	.5393	.4607
Condition H	13	.4397	.5603

somewhat more pronounced than were the differences reported in Table 8.2. Using stable-state estimates, the mean probabilities of a player one choice for subjects in Conditions *G, C,* and *H* are .6716, .5393, and .4397. The corresponding values are .6478, .4971, and .4323 when data from both pre-stabilization and stable-state are used to calculate the probabilities.

The distributions of the mean probability of a player one choice per subject in stable state also show a more pronounced differentiation when the three treatment conditions are compared. The three distributions are presented in Figure 8.3.

$\bar{P}_1$	Condition G	Condition C	Condition H
.96 – 1.	X		
.91 – .95			
.86 – .90	X	X	
.81 – .85	X	X	
.76 – .80		X	
.71 – .75	X		
.66 – .70			
.61 – .65	X	XX	X
.56 – .60	XX	XX	XXX
.51 – .55	X	XX	X
.46 – .50		X	X
.41 – .45			XXX
.36 – .40		X	X
.31 – .35		XX	X
.26 – .30	X		X
.21 – .25			
.16 – .20			
.11 – .15			
.06 – .10			
0 – .05		X	X
	N = 9	*N* = 14	*N* = 13

Figure 8.3 *Mean Player One Choices Per Subject After Stabilization in Experiment V.*

8.3 APPLICATION OF THE UNEQUAL ALPHA MODEL

In order to apply the choice model to situations in which the alpha ratios for two alternatives are unequal, it is necessary to obtain at least two independent sets of observations under varied π parameters.[1] These sets of observations are used to measure the alpha ratios associated with each alternative. The derivations of the equations of the unequal alpha model were presented in Chapter 3 and need not be repeated here. The final equations of the model for the two-alternative case are as follows:

$$P_1 = \tfrac{1}{4}(\pi_1\alpha_1 - \pi_2\alpha_2) + \tfrac{1}{2} \tag{1}$$

$$P_2 = 1 - P_1 \tag{2}$$

Using Conditions G and C as the measurement experiments, we obtain the following value of α_1:

$$\text{In Condition } G: \quad P_1 = .671605 = \tfrac{1}{4}(.8\alpha_1 - .2\alpha_2) + \tfrac{1}{2}$$
$$\text{In Condition } C: \quad P_1 = .539286 = \tfrac{1}{4}(.7\alpha_1 - .3\alpha_2) + \tfrac{1}{2}$$

Therefore:

$$(.671605 - .5)(4) = .8\alpha_1 - .2\alpha_2$$
$$(.539286 - .5)(4) = .7\alpha_1 - .3\alpha_2$$

Solving for α_1 we obtain:

$$\alpha_1 = \frac{\begin{vmatrix} .686420 & -.2 \\ .157144 & -.3 \end{vmatrix}}{\begin{vmatrix} .8 & -.2 \\ .7 & -.3 \end{vmatrix}}$$

$$= \frac{(-.3)(.686420) - (-.2)(.157144)}{(-.3)(.8) - (-.2)(.7)}$$

$$= 1.74497$$

Using the same procedures and Conditions G and C as the measurement experiments, we obtain the following value of α_2:

1. Note that using two measurement experiments in order to estimate the alpha ratios and predicting behavior in a third treatment condition satisfies all necessary conditions for the evaluation procedure to be considered noncircular.

In Condition G: $\quad P_1 = .671605 = \frac{1}{4}(.8\alpha_1 - .2\alpha_2) + \frac{1}{2}$

In Condition C: $\quad P_1 = .539286 = \frac{1}{4}(.7\alpha_1 - .3\alpha_2) + \frac{1}{2}$

Therefore:

$$(.671605 - .5)(4) = .8\alpha_1 - .2\alpha_2$$
$$(.539286 - .5)(4) = .7\alpha_1 - .3\alpha_2$$

Solving for α_2 we obtain:

$$\alpha_2 = \frac{\begin{vmatrix} .8 & .686420 \\ .7 & .157144 \end{vmatrix}}{\begin{vmatrix} .8 & -.2 \\ .7 & -.3 \end{vmatrix}}$$

$$= \frac{(.8)(.157144) - (.7)(.686420)}{(.8)(-.3) - (.7)(-.2)}$$

$$= 3.54779$$

With the estimates of α_1 and α_2 obtained above, it is possible to solve Eqs. (1) and (2) in order to obtain predictions for the stable-state choice strategy that subjects in Condition H will adopt if they are acting so as to maximize expected utility in their decision making. The predictions for the maximizing choice strategy (P_1 and P_2) for subjects in Condition H are generated as follows:

$$P_1 = \frac{1}{4}(\pi_1\alpha_1 - \pi_2\alpha_2) + \frac{1}{2}$$
$$= \frac{1}{4}[(.6)(1.74497) - (.4)(3.54779)] + \frac{1}{2}$$
$$= .4070$$
$$P_2 = 1 - P_1 = .5930$$

The predictions derived above can be evaluated through comparison with the observed stable-state probabilities of player one and player two choices made by subjects in Condition H. In Condition H, $\bar{P}_1 = .4397$ and $\bar{P}_2 = .5603$. The absolute difference between the observed and predicted choice strategies is .0327.

Given the data from the three treatment conditions it is possible to rotate measurement and prediction conditions and conduct three applications of the model. The results of all three applications are presented in Table 8.4. The results of the two additional applications together with the results discussed above demonstrate that the model predicts with a high degree of accuracy in all cases. Using Conditions G and H in order to predict Condition C, the

Table 8.4   *Results of Application of the Unequal Alpha Model*

Measurement experiments	Prediction experiment	Estimated α_1 and α_2	Predicted P_1 and P_2	Observed P_1 and P_2	|Discrepancy|
Conditions G and C	Condition H	1.74497	.4070	.4397	.0327
		3.54779	.5930	.5603	
Conditions G and H	Condition C	1.61386	.5557	.5393	.0164
		3.02336	.4443	.4607	
Conditions C and H	Condition G	1.35165	.6388	.6716	.0328
		2.63003	.3612	.3284	

model's predictions are accurate to an absolute discrepancy of .0164. In the final case, with C and H used to predict Condition G, the predictions are discrepant from the observed mean stable-state choice stategy by .0328.

8.4 SUMMARY

The unequal alpha form of the model was subjected to empirical test and applied in three instances. These applications represent only a single test of the model since the measurement and prediction conditions were rotated through all possible combinations. In comparison with the results of the application of the model to nonsocial decision making in the light-guessing experiment, the present application yields predictions which are not as accurate as those obtained by Siegel. In the unequal alpha tests that Siegel conducted, there were three events to be predicted, and the model yielded predictions which were on the average discrepant from the observed choice strategies by |.016|. For the present application, the average absolute discrepancy between predicted and observed choice strategies is .027.

The difference in the accuracy with which the model predicts behavior under the two test conditions is not great in an absolute sense. In addition, there are a number of points on which the two research programs varied that add to the difficulty in coming to any definite conclusion on the question of whether the model predicts better or worse in the social decision-making situation than it did in the nonsocial decision-making experiments. In the experiments conducted by Siegel, there were 18 subjects in each condition, while in the coalition game experiments there were an average of 12 subjects per condition. As has been shown previously, the accuracy with which the model predicts choice behavior varies directly with the size of the samples in measurement and test conditions. In addition, since in the light-guessing experiments there were three events to be predicted, a different procedure was used in order to estimate the alpha ratios. This procedure called for solving a set of overdetermined equations. The alternative estimation procedure together with the increased sample sizes should have resulted in somewhat more reliable estimates of the alpha ratio than were obtained with the procedure employed in the coalition researches.[2] This in turn could easily account for the observed difference in the model's predictive power.

2. The estimation of alpha ratios using an overdetermined equation procedure was not carried out in the application of the model to the coalition game research since the procedure would have required using all of the available data to obtain the alpha estimates. Employing these alpha estimates to predict choice behavior in the same treatment conditions from which the estimates were obtained would have compromised the status of the test procedure. (Estimation of alpha ratios through application of an overdetermined equation procedure will be considered in detail in Chapter 9.)

9

A Model for Freely
Interactive Behavior

This chapter reports the results of two tests of the generalization of the decision theory to the behavior of systems of freely interacting individuals. The phrase "system of freely interacting individuals" denotes a situation in which the true choices of each member of the interaction system are transmitted to all other members of the system. The research setting was therefore a truly interacting coalition game with three human players in which the experimenter introduced *no control* over the information subjects received about the choices of the other participants in his game.

It should be understood that an interaction system of the type described above is freely interactive only with regard to the transmission of the true decisions of all the players in the game. The payoffs an individual received for alternative coalitions were fixed, and hence there was no bargaining over the division of rewards. Players were not permitted to conduct negotiations leading to side payments; nor could they attempt to influence the choices of the other players through transmission of offers to enter into guaranteed, long-term alliances. Further, the messages that players received were restricted to the same set as was used in the highly controlled experiments reported previously. (On each iteration of the game subjects received one and only one of the four messages discussed in Section 5.2.)

Players did, however, have open to them the possibility of establishing a form of communication with the other individuals in their game by signaling their desires through consistent action. It was therefore possible for a player in the games reported below to communicate a desire to enter into a permanent alliance through consistent selection of a second individual and for knowledge of this desire to affect the choice strategy of the second player. This possibility represents a major departure from the conditions of the previous researches since, in the earlier experiments, the behavior of the robots was unalterable and therefore subjects could not establish permanent alliances even if they so desired.

The generalization of the theory to freely interactive settings represents a considerable extension of its scope. The qualities of the social situation to which the theory will be applied are greatly different from those to which it has been applied previously. In a situation in which an individual plays against two programmed robots, the variables that can affect his behavior may be minimally controlled by the experimenter. At least, all subjects in a given treatment condition hear the same instructions, are offered the same payoffs for alternative coalitions, and are then presented with identical sequences of choices by the two robots. Although in a freely interactive situation the first two factors can still be controlled, the inability to control the possibilities for interaction, and therefore a substantial number of potentially causal variables, results in a much "richer" research setting.

Consider for example the potential effects of the first information an individual receives about the behavior of the other players. The information is in the form of a message reporting their choices on the first iteration of the game. If a subject selects his monetarily preferred coalition partner and happens to form a coalition on his first attempt, he might easily feel that it would be wise to pursue a course of action leading to establishment of an "easy" permanent alliance with this friendly player. If, however, on the first play the subject selects his economically preferred alternative, this player does not choose him, and the other player does, he might feel that it is wise to attempt to form an alliance with his less preferred coalition partner since he can win a small amount of money through this course of action. Finally, if no coalition forms on the first play, it could lead to a period in which all players shift choices in an attempt to form any alliance and are less loyal throughout the duration of the game. Although all of the above-mentioned first trial outcomes are possible in games played with robots, the fixed pattern of subsequent robot choices might tend to induce greater similarity in the behavior of subjects than would be obtained in experiments in which free interaction is permitted.

A second major difference between robot-interactive and free-interactive games relates to considerations of equity. In the highly controlled experiments, subjects cannot establish permanent alliances even if they so desire. That is, the robots are not responsive to invitations to form permanent coalitions. In a free interactive situation, it is possible for two players to unite to the detriment of the third. Given that under free interactive conditions permanent alliances are actually within the realm of possible outcomes, it would be quite important if this change in the structure of the research situation did not affect the behavior of players in the game. Accurate predictions under these conditions would indicate that an individual's assignment of utility to equity is independent of the characteristics of the setting in which the individual subsequently finds himself. Note that the preceding assertion is not contradictory to the argument that the utility a subject assigns to equity is a function of the orientation he is given in the instructions for the game. We propose that given some magnitude of utility for equity induced by a set of instructions, if the instructions are held constant and the possibilities for interaction in the subsequent experiment are altered, it will not affect the individual's utility for equity. That is, an individual's desire for equity will remain fixed even in the event of the possibility of formation of a permanent alliance. If this condition holds, it will be possible to predict an individual's behavior given utility estimates obtained under a set of conditions that are substantially different from the conditions of the situation in which his behavior is to be predicted.

There are four aspects to the report of the application of the theory to free interaction. The first consists of a discussion of the generalization itself. The second segment reports the estimation of alpha ratios using a different method than has been employed previously and a re-analysis of the data from the robot-interactive experiments in light of the re-estimated alpha ratios. The third and fourth segments report two tests of the generalization to free interactive behavior.

9.1 ON THE GENERALIZATION TO FREE INTERACTIVE BEHAVIOR

The formal generalization of the theory to the behavior of systems of freely interacting individuals was presented in Section 4.3. The aim of this section is to discuss the steps leading to the generalization, the substantive meaning of the generalization, and the strategy that will be used in order to test its power.

The manner in which the generalization of the theory was arrived at is intimately related to the fact that the individual decision-making theory had earlier been formalized as a mathematical model. In fact, it might easily be argued that it would have been difficult to recognize that the individual decision theory could be extended to a theory of the behavior of interaction systems and virtually impossible to arrive at precise predictions for system behavior without starting from a *formal* model of individual decision making. The reason for the greater ease with which the potential of the theory could be recognized is the greater conceptual power made available through the device of formalization. Once formalized it was possible to operate on the axioms of the theory using the rules of the formal system to which the theory had been coordinated.

It has been argued (Berger et al., 1962) that due to differences in the primary goal of their formalization, mathematical models should be regarded as varying in type. Further, in order to understand the role of formal models in the development of substantive knowledge of social behavior it is necessary to understand the purpose for which a model was constructed. Berger et al. identify three distinct uses and therefore three distinct types of formal models in social science. They consider explicational, representational, and theoretical construct models. The use of explicational models is to render precise one or more concepts. An example of an explicational model is Cartwright and Harary's (1956) formalization of Heider's concept of balance. The second reason for constructing a formal model is to represent in "as precise and formally simple manner as possible, a specific type of observed social phenomenon" (p. 37). Cohen's (1963) model of behavior in the Asch conformity experiment is an example of a representational model. The third type of formal model is identified as a theoretical construct model. The principal goal of this type of formalization "is to provide a direct means of developing a general explanatory theory which formally accounts for a variety of observed processes" (p. 67). The formal model of the decision-making theory is an example of a theoretical construct model.

The typology created by Berger et al. clearly rests on the recognition that models are only heuristics. They are created to serve some purpose and are only valuable insofar as they contribute to the advance of substantive knowledge, whether through clarification of the meaning of a major concept, through reduction of a vast amount of data so that its regularities can be identified and described by a relatively simple formal statement, or through permitting translation of the substantive axioms of a theory into a formal system that permits manipulation of the theory's axioms by applying a relatively simple set of rules. Most social scientists who are more interested in understanding behavior than in being mathematically elegant for its own sake seem to subscribe to the idea that formalizations are useful for the general purpose of "making explicit the logical structure of a set of assertions" (Berger et al., 1962, p. 1). For example, in discussing his choice of a mode of formal representation of certain causal theories in his writing on the construction of social theories, Stinchcombe (1968) states:

The linear graph treatment of complex causal theories has the advantage of representing the overall structure of a theory in an intuitively easy fashion, much easier to understand than a statement of the same theory in terms of a system of linear equations. The algebra of such graphs is often easier to manipulate to get a solution than the equivalent algebra of systems of linear equations (p. 131).[1]

In terms of the typology of formal models proposed by Berger et al. the decision theory developed by Siegel is a theoretical construct model. It is a formal representation, that is, a precise specification of the substantive theory of decision making that Siegel proposed. The basic substantive axioms of the theory dealt with the idea of maximization of expected utility in decision making and the manner in which utilities associated with a particular choice could be combined. The formal model of this theory was a precise statement of how the theoretically important variables were related.

To understand how it is possible to move from the individual decision theory to a formulation for the behavior of interaction systems, it is necessary to follow a series of steps that begins with the intellectual realization that it should be possible to apply the theory to interaction systems and ends with a manipulation of the formal model that yields predictions for the behavior of the interaction system under specified experimental conditions.

The realization that the theory should apply to freely interactive systems was reached through consideration of the concrete setting chosen for research on individual social decision making. It should be remembered that the coalition game was originally chosen simply as a convenient setting in which to conduct research on social decision making. Toward this end, we analyzed the game situation in terms of its components of choice and bargaining. We proposed that if the bargaining aspects of the situation could be controlled, an individual in the game could be reasonably conceptualized as being faced with a binary decision problem that involved considerations of the probabilities of actions by the other participants in the game, his marginal utility for payoffs for alternative coalitions, and his marginal utility for the welfare of the other players in the game. The general decision-making theory developed by Siegel and his associates was applied to this decision problem and found to predict exceedingly well.

1. The aim of this discussion is by no means to instruct in the rules of theory construction nor the place of formal models in behavioral research. These ends are admirably accomplished by books such as Berger, Cohen, Snell, and Zelditch's *Types of Formalization in Small-Group Research* (1962) and Stinchcombe's *Constructing Social Theories* (1968). The aim here is simply to point out that without a formal structure for the decision theory it would have been exceedingly difficult to arrive at precise predictions for individual behavior, the generalization to the behavior of interaction systems or, for that matter, any nonobvious theorem that followed from the substantive axioms of the theory.

The experimental situation created to test the individual decision theory was one that simulated a coalition game by using robots for two of the three players. In this way, the behavior of all but the human player could be controlled, and the behavior of the human player could be studied. The equations that were expected to yield predictions for the maximizing strategy subjects would adopt under equal alpha conditions were:

$$P_{1,2} = \frac{\alpha}{4}(\pi_{2,1} - \pi_{3,1}) + .5$$

$$P_{1,3} = \frac{\alpha}{4}(\pi_{3,1} - \pi_{2,1}) + .5$$

With player one as the human subject and players two and three as the robots, the notation for the equations is read as follows:

$P_{1,x}$ = the probability with which player one chooses robot x and
$\pi_{x,1}$ = the probability with which robot x chooses the subject.

If a coalition game involving three human players is considered it can be easily understood how relations between players are represented in the choice equations. Consider the player number one discussed above to be in a three-person coalition game. The probabilities with which he is chosen by the other players correspond to the $\pi_{2,1}$ and $\pi_{3,1}$ terms in the choice equations. Half of the inputs to player one come from player two and half come from player three. If either player two or player three is taken as the focal position, the same relation holds. Half of any player's outputs ($P_{x,y}$ or $P_{x,z}$) constitute half of each of the other two players' inputs.

Since P and π values are equivalent for players in interaction it is obvious that the π terms may be substituted with appropriate P terms without changing the meaning of the equations. These substitutions serve to formally interconnect the choice equations for three players who are in interaction. The manner in which they are interconnected reproduces their relations in the game.

The equations that predict player one's maximizing choice strategy may now be written as:

$$P_{1,2} = \frac{\alpha}{4}(P_{2,1} - P_{3,1}) + .5$$

$$P_{1,3} = \frac{\alpha}{4}(P_{3,1} - P_{2,1}) + .5$$

The equations for player two and three's maximizing strategies may, of course, be written in a corresponding fashion.

The next step in generalizing the model is to rewrite the equations for individual decision making for all players as a system of linear equations.

The system of equations that results from this operation is:

$$4P_{1,2} - \alpha_{1,2}P_{2,1} + \alpha_{1,3}P_{3,1} = 2$$

$$\alpha_{2,1}P_{1,2} - 4P_{2,1} + \alpha_{2,3}P_{3,1} = \alpha_{2,3} - 2$$

$$\alpha_{3,1}P_{1,2} + \alpha_{3,2}P_{2,1} + 4P_{3,1} = \alpha_{3,1} - \alpha_{3,2} + 2$$

Given proper manipulation, it is possible to generate predictions for the choice behavior of each member of the interaction system. For example, in a free interactive situation the probability with which player one should select player two if he wishes to maximize his expected utility is:

$$P_{1,2} = \frac{-32 + \alpha_{2,3}\alpha_{3,2}(2 - \alpha_{1,3}) + \alpha_{1,2}\alpha_{2,3}(3 - \alpha_{3,1}) + 8(\alpha_{1,3} - \alpha_{1,2}) + 2\alpha_{1,3}(2\alpha_{3,1} - \alpha_{3,2}) + \alpha_{1,2}(\alpha_{2,3})^2}{-64 + 4\alpha_{2,3}\alpha_{3,2} + 4\alpha_{1,2}\alpha_{2,1} + 4\alpha_{1,3}\alpha_{3,1} - \alpha_{1,2}\alpha_{2,3}\alpha_{3,1} - \alpha_{1,3}\alpha_{3,2}\alpha_{2,1}}$$

The rules of the formal system to which the theory was coordinated permitted manipulation of equations for individual choice behavior such that the relations between players in free interactive coalition games could be represented. In addition, it was possible to define all unknowns in the equations in terms of the alpha constants. This resulted in a situation in which predictions could be derived for the maximizing choice behavior of each member of the system. This is obviously equivalent to a prediction of the equilibrium point that the system would attain.

Since, in addition to the quantities to be predicted, the final equations for individual and system behavior contain only one unknown term, alpha, the solution of the equations is straighforward if a value for alpha can be introduced. Fortunately, it is a relatively simple task to obtain an estimate for alpha that is independent of the data to be used to test the model's predictions. The estimates for alpha values that will be introduced into the equations will be obtained from the data generated in the robot-interactive experiments. The method through which these estimates are produced is discussed in Section 9.2.

Given the formal generalization of the theory and an appropriate procedure for estimation of alpha ratios, the model yields predictions for the equilibrium behavior of both individuals and interaction systems. The substantive theory that leads to these predictions assumes all participants in the interaction system can be treated as if they act so as to maximize expected utility in their decision making. In an attempt not to lose sight of the relationship between the substantive theory and the model's predictions for the behavior of interaction systems, the following discussion attempts to demonstrate how the model arrives at its equilibrium predictions by treating the dynamic system described by the linear equations in a number of discrete steps.

Consider the three-person coalition game with the structure represented in Figure 9.1. In this game player one receives 10 cents if he is able to form a coalition with player two and five cents for a coalition with player three. Players two and three are each paid five cents for any coalition that they are able to form. The structure of the game suggests that player one will be relatively more desirous of forming coalitions with player two than with player three and that players two and three will be indifferent between alternative coalitions.

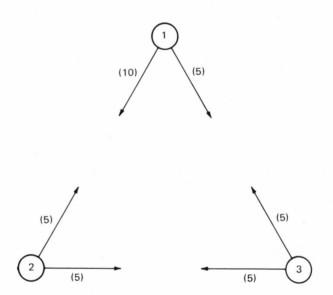

Figure 9.1 *A Free Interactive Coalition Game Structure.* The notation for figures representing game structures should be read as follows: Ⓧ defines a player: Ⓧ (5) defines the payoff that player *X* receives for a coalition with the player indicated by the directed line.

In order to demonstrate the mutual adjustment process that leads to the equilibrium point it is convenient to make a set of reasonable, albeit arbitrary, assumptions about how players in the game described in Figure 9.1 will initially behave. Given these assumptions about initial behavior dispositions and the theory's substantive and formal axioms, it is possible to "operate" the system in a number of discrete steps. For the assumptions about initial dispositions it is reasonable to suppose that for economic reasons player one will be oriented to choose player two rather than player three. We shall assume that for the first few repetitions of the game he chooses player two with probability one and player three with probability zero. We also shall assume that players two and three are initially indifferent between alternative coalitions for economic reasons (they are each paid five cents for either possible coalition), and will each therefore be affected by the probabilities with which they are chosen by their potential partners.

Given these initial assumptions we can treat the system as operating in discrete steps until equilibrium is reached. That is, we can treat the system as if there were periods in which one player's behavior is fixed and the other players adjust to his outputs. During the next period, the first player modifies his choice strategy so that he maximizes expected utility with respect to his inputs from the other members of the system. The process can be repeated until a stable set of inputs and outputs results. Note that the assumption of discrete steps is made strictly for explicational purposes. In fact, the theory assumes that the mutual adjustment process is continuous for all members of the system.

Using the suggested assumptions about initial behavior dispositions for players in the game represented in Figure 9.1 and the restriction that for the first few repetitions of the game player one will employ a fixed strategy, the model can be applied and the maximizing choice strategy for players two and three can be specified. The maximizing strategies are arrived at by solving the system of linear equations after introducing appropriate alpha values and player one's predetermined strategy $(P_{1,2} = 1, P_{1,3} = 0)^2$. If players two and three act so as to maximize utility in their decision making they will adopt the following strategies:

$$P_{2,1} = .8586 \qquad P_{2,3} = .1414$$
$$P_{3,1} = .3886 \qquad P_{3,2} = .6114$$

Assume that players two and three adopt the maximizing strategies specified above and maintain them as long as player one holds to his 1-0 outputs. Confronted with these behaviors on the parts of the other members of the interaction system, the theory predicts that player one will, if necessary, modify his choice strategy so that it maximizes expected utility. If, with respect to the behaviors of players two and three specified above, the 1-0 strategy maximizes player one's expected utility, he would be predicted to maintain that choice distribution. Using the equation that was employed to predict behavior in the robot-interactive experiments, we can determine player one's maximizing strategy with respect to the behavior of players two and three as follows:

$$P_{1,2} = \tfrac{1}{4}(\alpha_{1,2}P_{2,1} - \alpha_{1,3}P_{3,1}) + .5$$
$$= \tfrac{1}{4}[(3.02485)(.8586) - (1.58258)(.3886)] + .5$$
$$= .9955$$
$$P_{1,3} = 1 - P_{1,2} = .0045$$

---

2. The alpha values used in this discussion are estimated in Section 9.2.

Since player one's maximizing strategy is discrepant from his pre-determined, 1-0 choice distribution, we shall assume that he eventually modifies his original strategy and moves to the maximizing outputs. Given player one's new outputs, it would be expected that players two and three would adjust their behaviors in response to player one's change. The model would predict that players two and three would move to the following strategies in order to maximize utility:

$$P_{2,1} = .8514 \qquad P_{2,3} = .1486$$
$$P_{3,1} = .3857 \qquad P_{3,2} = .6143$$

Once players two and three adjust their outputs to player one's modified behavior the model may be employed to predict how player one will react. His maximizing strategy with respect to the new outputs of players two and three is:

$$P_{1,2} = \tfrac{1}{4}(\alpha_{1,2}P_{2,1} - \alpha_{1,3}P_{3,1}) + .5$$
$$= \tfrac{1}{4}[(3.02485)(.8514) - (1.58258)(.3857)] + .5$$
$$= .9912$$
$$P_{1,3} = 1 - P_{1,2} = .0088$$

If the process of discrete modifications of choice behavior outlined above were to be repeated for 10 additional iterations, the three players would be choosing one another with the following probabilities:

$$P_{1,2} = .9567 \qquad P_{1,3} = .0433$$
$$P_{2,1} = .7893 \qquad P_{2,3} = .2107$$
$$P_{3,1} = .3610 \qquad P_{3,2} = .6390$$

An additional 10 iterations of the process results in the following maximizing strategies:

$$P_{1,2} = .9340 \qquad P_{1,3} = .0660$$
$$P_{2,1} = .7528 \qquad P_{2,3} = .2472$$
$$P_{3,1} = .3465 \qquad P_{3,2} = .6535$$

The iterative process could be continued until the interaction system reaches an equilibrium point—the point at which all players are maximizing expected utility with respect to the behaviors of the other participants in the game. Once having arrived at the equilibrium point the model predicts that all players will indefinitely maintain the specified choice strategies. For the interaction system under discussion, the equilibrium point to which the system will move is:

$$P_{1,2} = .8896 \qquad P_{1,3} = .1104$$
$$P_{2,1} = .6817 \qquad P_{2,3} = .3183$$
$$P_{3,1} = .3183 \qquad P_{3,2} = .6817$$

The equilibrium point described by the iterative process is the same point that could be directly described by solving the system of simultaneous linear equations for the generalized choice model.

The purpose of the preceding discussion was to demonstrate how, through a series of mutual adjustments by participants, the model predicts the interaction system will move to an equilibrium point. The method used to demonstrate this adjustment process was designed to be illustrative rather than necessarily substantively correct in detail, since certain assumptions about alternating periods of fixed and changing behavior were introduced.

9.2 ESTIMATION OF UTILITY RATIOS USING ALL AVAILABLE DATA

Since in the two experiments to be reported in this chapter subjects are in interaction with other individuals rather than with robot players, the experiments are substantially different from all of the previously reported researches. In addition to differences in the concrete settings of the experiments, the current researches are distinguished from the earlier experiments in that different sets of subjects were employed in the experiments reported below. No subject participated in more than one treatment condition for any of the researches reported in this book. All subjects were, however, drawn from a common population.

The model's ability to predict the behavior of freely interacting systems of individuals rests on the success with which measurements are made of the utilities of the commodities that each member of the system considers in his decision making. It has been shown that if estimates of these utilities can be obtained, it is possible to generate predictions for how the interaction system will behave given only these estimates and knowledge of the payoffs each member of the system is offered for his alternative coalitions.

In order to preserve the validity of the procedure used to test the model's power, it is necessary to obtain estimates of the relevant utilities (alpha ratios) that are independent of data used to test the model. This was accomplished in the robot-interactive experiments through the procedure of using one set of data with which to estimate alpha ratios and a second set against which to test the model's predictions. For the test of the model under free-interactive conditions the estimates of alpha ratios will be obtained from the data generated by subjects who participated in the robot-interactive experiments.

In this way, no data from the free-interactive experiments will be used in generating predictions for the behavior of the interaction system.

The data from the robot-interactive experiments permit alpha estimates to be obtained for two different sets of experimental conditions. These have been referred to as equal and unequal alpha conditions. Equal alpha conditions denote an experimental situation in which the subject is offered five cents if he is able to form either of his alternative coalitions. Unequal alpha conditions denotes an experimental situation in which the subject is offered five cents for formation of one of his possible coalitions and 10 cents if he is able to form the other coalition. Both the equal and unequal alpha experiments from which data will be used to estimate alpha ratios for the free-interactive researches were conducted with a low equity manipulation.

The alpha estimates that can be obtained from these data permit predictions to be generated for any free-interactive coalition games, providing three conditions are met. These are (1) that the pre-game instructions to subjects incorporate a low equity manipulation similar to the one employed in the robot-interactive experiments, (2) that subjects are offered either five cents for each coalition or five cents for one coalition and 10 cents for the other, and (3) that subjects are male and believe that the other participants in their game are also males. Given realization of these conditions, it will be possible to predict interaction in games in which all players are offered identical payoffs for their possible coalitions or games in which some players are offered equal payoffs for alternative coalitions and other players are offered unequal payoffs for forming coalitions.

The data generated by male subjects in Conditions A and B of Experiment I (the equal alpha experiment) and Conditions C, G, and H of Experiment V (the unequal alpha experiment) provide the basic information from which alpha ratios will be estimated. Since there were differences in the π parameters used in the various treatment conditions within each experiment, it is not possible to simply combine data from Conditions A and B or Conditions C, G, and H and re-estimate the necessary alpha ratios. For example, Conditions A and B were both run under equal alpha conditions; subjects were offered five cents for forming either coalition in both treatment conditions. In Condition A, however, subjects were chosen by the robot players with probabilities of .70 and .30, while in Condition B they were chosen with probabilities of .60 and .40.

The original procedure used to generate predictions for behavior in Experiment I was first to estimate alpha from the data obtained from Condition A and predict behavior in Condition B and then to reverse the procedure, using B to estimate alpha and predict behavior in Condition A. For Experiment V, the unequal alpha experiment, it was necessary to use two measurement conditions in order to estimate the alpha ratio for each of the payoffs. For this experiment α_1 denoted the utility ratio associated with the five-cent coalition and α_2 denoted the ratio associated with the 10-cent payoff. The procedure of using only a portion of the available data with which to estimate alpha ratios resulted in two slightly different estimates for equal alpha conditions and three differing pairs of estimates for the unequal alpha conditions. The results of these estimating procedures are summarized in Table 9.1.

Table 9.1 *Estimates of Alpha from Robot-Interactive Experiments**

Measurement condition(s)	Number of subjects	Payoffs for coalitions	Alpha estimate
Condition A	22	$a_1 = a_2 = \$.05$	$\alpha_1 = \alpha_2 = 3.49495$
Condition B	21	$a_1 = a_2 = \$.05$	$\alpha_1 = \alpha_2 = 3.50000$
Conditions C and G	14 + 9	$a_1 = \$.05$	$\alpha_1 = 1.74497$
		$a_2 = \$.10$	$\alpha_2 = 3.54779$
Conditions G and H	9 + 13	$a_1 = \$.05$	$\alpha_1 = 1.61386$
		$a_2 = \$.10$	$\alpha_2 = 3.02336$
Conditions C and H	14 + 13	$a_1 = \$.05$	$\alpha_1 = 1.35165$
		$a_2 = \$.10$	$\alpha_2 = 2.63003$

*The alpha estimates reported here are generated from the stable-state behavior of subjects in the various conditions. The stabilization points were selected on the basis of inspection of the data.

The estimates reported in Table 9.1 reveal that although there are some differences in the estimates obtained using different subsets of the available data, there is notable consistency across estimates. For example, the two completely independent estimates of alpha ratios under equal payoff conditions differ by only .00505 (in Condition *A*, alpha equals 3.49495, and in Condition *B* the estimate is 3.50000). For unequal alpha conditions it is necessary to use two of the three treatment conditions in order to obtain a single pair of estimates. The resulting estimates for α_1 are 1.74497, 1.61386, and 1.35165. For α_2 the estimates are 3.54779, 3.02336, and 2.63003.

In order to predict behavior in free-interactive situations it is necessary to obtain a single estimate for alpha under equal payoff conditions and a single pair of estimates for α_1 and α_2 under unequal payoff conditions. It is reasonable to regard the differences in estimates that are obtained from subsets of the available data as reflecting random variation arising from sampling error. The immediate problem therefore becomes one of obtaining alpha estimates based on all available data. In his work on the choice theory, Siegel (1964) developed a method for estimating alpha from more than the minimum necessary data. The method essentially consists in constructing a set of overdetermined simultaneous equations and solving for the best estimate of alpha. This method was applied to the data generated in the robot-interactive experiments with the following results.[3] Using all data from Conditions A and B, the best estimate of alpha under equal, five-cent payoff conditions is a value of 3.49663. Using all data from Conditions C, G, and H the best estimate for α_1 is 1.58258 (a_1 = \$.05) and for α_2 (a_2 = \$.10) it is 3.02485.

For the purpose of predicting behavior under free-interactive conditions these alpha estimates may, of course, be regarded as being completely independent of the data against which the theory's predictions will be evaluated. Although these estimates are not independent of the robot-interactive experiments, it is interesting to observe the predictive power of the model if new predictions are generated for the various experimental conditions. If the newly obtained alpha estimates are more nearly correct approximations of the true utility ratios, they should generate more accurate predictions in every case. Note that more accurate predictions in every case are not guaranteed simply because the data from the conditions to be predicted

Table 9.2 *Comparison of the Model's Accuracy Using Two Alpha Estimation Procedures*

Experiment	Treatment condition	Absolute discrepancy using independent estimation	Absolute discrepancy using nonindependent estimation
I	A	.0005	.0002
I	B	.0003	.0003
V	C	.0164	.0108
V	G	.0328	.0063
V	H	.0327	.0048

contributed to the estimation procedure. Although predictions should on the average be more accurate using the second estimation procedure, it is possible that the estimates obtained in this manner could result in less accurate predictions in some of the applications of the model. In generating the equal alpha estimate, Condition A accounted for 51% of the data used in the estimation procedure and Condition B accounted for the remaining 49%. In generating the unequal alpha estimates Condition C contributed 39% of the data, Condition G contributed 25%, and Condition H the remaining 36% of the basic data.

3. The procedure by which the alpha estimates are obtained using more than minimum data is described in detail in Chapter 5 of *Choice Strategy and Utility*, Siegel et al. (1964). The computations leading to the estimates reported in this section are presented in Appendix I.

Table 9.2 reports the results of a comparison of the accuracy with which the robot-interactive experiments can be predicted with the old and new alpha estimates. The result is that the predictions generated with the re-estimated alpha ratios are in every case as or more accurate than those estimated with the independent estimation procedure.

9.3 INTERACTION IN GROUPS WITH INTERCHANGEABLE STRUCTURAL POSITIONS

The first application of the choice theory to decision making in a freely interactive social situation was conducted in a setting in which all subjects occupied structurally identical positions, that is, in a setting in which all subjects received identical payoffs for alternative coalitions and were interconnected so that each player's high payoff alternative was another player's low payoff alternative. (The design of the research setting will be discussed in detail below.)

In order to ensure basic comparability with the researches from which the alpha estimates were obtained, it was necessary to hold certain experimental conditions constant. The following are the characteristics of the experiments which were preserved in the transition from a computer-controlled environment to one in which the computer functioned primarily as a device for transmission of information between players.

Physical Setting. The physical environment in which the research was conducted was identical to that employed previously. Subjects were initially briefed in a large room in groups of either six or nine individuals. Therefore, the conditions of anonymity attained in the robot-interactive experiments were maintained in the free-interactive experiments. Subjects knew that they would be playing with two other males but could not determine the identity of the other players in their particular game. After the briefing, participants were taken into separate rooms from which the game was to be played.

Instructions. The procedures used in the free-interactive experiments were identical to those employed in the experiments from which the alpha estimates were obtained. The free-interactive experiments were conducted using the same low equity manipulation as was employed in Conditions *A*, *B*, *C*, *G*, and *H* of the coalition game researches. The text of the instructions is reported in Section 5.2. When subjects were taken to the smaller rooms, the instructions for the use of the teletypes were repeated. An instruction sheet, posted on the teletype, informed the subject of the payoff he would get for each of his alternative coalitions. It was also made clear to subjects that they had no information about the payoffs the other players received for coalitions with them. Each subject was told that the other players in the game might be getting "more, the same amount, or less money" for forming coalitions with him. These instructions were identical to those given to subjects in the robot-interactive games.

Payoffs. Within the limits imposed by the available estimates for alpha ratios it is possible to construct numerous coalition game structures. The measured utility ratios restrict the possible games that can be considered to cases in which players are offered either five cents for each alternative coalition (a 5-5 position) or five cents for one alternative and 10 cents for the other (a 5-10 position). Given this restriction, however, the experimenter is free to construct games in any manner he desires. The game structure may be varied from a situation in which all players occupy 5-5 payoff positions to a situation in which all players occupy 5-10 positions. Given these basic game structures, the investigator has the freedom to interconnect payoff positions in any manner. For example, it is possible to generate predictions for behavior in a game in which there are two 5-10 players and one 5-5 player and the two 5-10 players are interconnected such that each one is the other's 10-cent alternative. The model will also predict choice behavior in games in which there are two 5-10 players and one 5-5 player and for each of the 5-10 players it is the case that his 10-cent alternative is one of the equally desirable choice options open to the 5-5 player.

Communication. As noted previously, the form of communication between players was not altered between the controlled and interactive experiments. The content of messages was fixed, even though the true choices of all three players determined the messages they each received rather than having their content determined only by each player's own choice and a predetermined schedule of robot choices. For example, if player one chose player two, two happened to reciprocate his choice, and player three did not choose player one, player one would receive a message which read, "You were chosen by player two. You won five [or 10] cents."

Since the model can be used to predict behavior in any game structure providing that the alternative payoffs offered to a subject are either five cents for each coalition (a 5-5 position) or five cents for one and 10 cents for the other coalition (a 5-10 position), it is possible to create a variety of different game structures. Some of the possible structures are trivial since intuitive predictions for how the interaction system will behave are similar to the predictions that the theory generates. For example, consider games with the structures defined in Figure 9.2.

In game I of Figure 9.2 the three players occupy identical structural positions since they are all offered the same payoffs for their possible coalitions and are interconnected in a manner such that all theoretically relevant conditions are equivalent for all players. Consider player one. He is offered

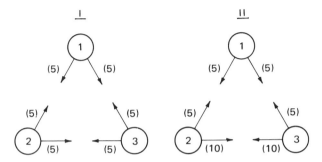

Figure 9.2 *Two Coalition Games with Uninteresting Structures.* The notation should be read as follows: ⊗ defines a player; ⊗＿(5)→ defines the payoff that player X receives for a coalition with the player indicated by the directed line.

five cents for a coalition with either player two or player three. For a coalition with player one, players two and three are each offered a payoff of five cents. Observe that from their viewpoints, all players in the game face identical decision problems, and the factors that the theory predicts will affect the decisions of the players with whom each is interacting are identical for players in all positions. Under the conditons of game I, the theory would predict that a player in any position would be indifferent between alternative coalitions, all players would behave in identical fashions, and all coalitions are equally likely. This corresponds to intuitive expectations for the behavior of the system and can be predicted from any of the traditional coalition theories.

Game II of Figure 9.2 is somewhat more interesting since there are two unique structural positions in the game and the behavior of an individual is predicted to be considerably affected by his place in the structure. Players two and three occupy structural positions that are equivalent and are different from the structural position occupied by player one. The differences between structural positions are in terms of both the player's payoffs for forming alternative coalitions and the factors affecting the players with whom he interacts. Players two and three are each in 5-10 payoff positions and player one is in a 5-5 position. In addition, the manner in which the players are interconnected makes the structural positions of players two and three identical and further differentiates their situation from the decision problem faced by player one. From player one's viewpoint, the game is one in which he is indifferent between alternative coalitions with regard to payoffs, and he is likely to find that neither of his potential coalition partners are eager to form coalitions with him. For players two and three the situation is quite different. Each player has a clear, monetarily induced preference for a particular coalition and each will find that his preferred coalition partner is equally desirous of forming coalitions with him. Players two and three are in a situation in which each one is the other's preferred alternative. It is intuitively obvious, and predicted from the choice theory, that these two players will form an alliance, and although equity considerations might lead to an occasional coalition with player one, the two-three alliance will dominate the game. It is also both intuitively obvious and formally predictable that since players in the number one position must register a choice on each iteration of the game, are indifferent between alternative coalitions, and are chosen with equal likelihood by players in positions two and three, they will choose players two and three with equal probabilities $(P_{1,2} = P_{1,3} = .5)$.

The ideal circumstances under which to conduct meaningful tests of the generalized choice theory would be to create game structures in which the behavior of each of the players is counter intuitive and not predictable from any of the traditional coalition theories. Unfortunately, this is not possible since choice behavior will tend to be compatible with predictions derived from a straightforward economic analysis of an individual's decision problem. It is possible, however, to construct situations in which, although it may be possible to predict the subjects' general choice tendencies from a naïve economic analysis, their precise optimizing strategies cannot be arrived at without the formal model. The first test of the generalized theory was conducted in a game of this type in which all players occupied structurally interchangeable positions.

In order for structural positions in a game to be interchangeable they must be equivalent with respect to three factors. First, all players must be given pre-game instructions that include the same equity manipulation. Second, all players must be offered the same payoffs for alternative coalitions (either 5-5 or 5-10). Finally, the theoretically relevant variables that affect the choices of the individuals with whom the player is in interaction must be the same.

With regard to the third point, consider a game with three players, X, Y, and Z. In order for X and Y to be in structurally interchangeable positions it would have to be the case that they were each interacting with sets of individuals who had identical motivations to form coalitions with them. In this game, player X is in interaction with players Y and Z, and player Y is in interaction with players X and Z. If a coalition with player X yielded five cents to both players Y and Z, while a coalition with Y yielded five cents to X

and 10 cents to *Z*, *X* and *Y* could not be considered to be in interchangeable positions. Player *X* represents a five-cent coalition to both of his potential partners, while a coalition with *Y* pays five cents to one of the individuals with whom he is in interaction and 10 cents to the other. Clearly, the economic motivations affecting *Y* and *Z*'s choices of *X* will be different from the economic motivations affecting *X* and *Z*'s choices of *Y*.

Given the restrictions cited above and the payoff positions for which alpha ratios have been measured (5-5 and 5-10), there are only two game structures with completely interchangeable positions. One is a game in which all players have 5-5 payoff positions, and the other is one in which all players have 5-10 payoff positions and are interconnected in a certain fashion. The first game structure was represented in Figure 9.2 and discussed previously. It was classified as trivial since predictions for the dynamics of the system are intuitively obvious and predictable from traditional coalition theories.

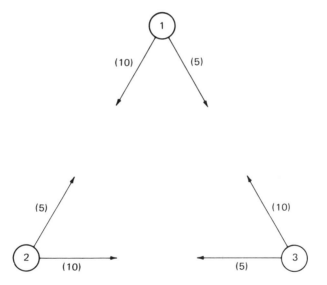

Figure 9.3 *A Coalition Game Structure with Interchangeable Positions.* The notation should be read as follows: ⊗ defines a player; ⊗ (5) → defines the payoff that player *X* receives for a coalition with the player indicated by the directed line.

In the second game structure (represented in Figure 9.3), each player is paid five cents for forming one of his possible coalitions and 10 cents if he is able to form the alternative coalition. The players are interconnected such that for each one it is the case that his 10-cent alternative corresponds to another player's five-cent alternative. Each member of the interaction system is therefore faced with a choice problem in which he can attempt to form a relatively valuable coalition with an individual who is not motivated to ally with him or he can enter into coalitions with an individual who is very desirous of an alliance but with whom a coalition is less valuable. This game structure provides a setting in which the predictions for the dynamics of the interaction system are not obvious and was therefore selected as the first research setting in which to test the generalized decision theory.

Since the game under consideration is truly interactive, certain complex behavior patterns are possible. For example, during some segment of a game the following sequence of events might occur. Assume that players one and two have formed an alliance that has remained stable for five trials. For this alliance, player one receives 10 cents per coalition and player two makes only five cents. Under these circumstances it is likely that player three (who gets 10 cents for a coalition with player one and five cents for a coalition with player two) will have discovered earlier in the game that player one has little interest in forming coalitions with him while player two is eager for an alliance; player three will therefore set about to break the player one-two alliance by consistently choosing player two. Player two now finds himself in a position to move from a relatively unrewarding alliance with player one to a profitable alliance with player three. Observe that if player two defects from the one-two alliance and player one is wise, he will use a strategy identical to the one just described in his attempt to break the two-three alliance.

The type of strategic considerations outlined above are illustrative of the complex interaction situation that even this simple game becomes when an attempt is made to analyze the set of motivations and conditions leading to a particular choice, the reactions to the choice, and the reactions to the reaction to the event. The argument of the theory is that these unique sequences of events may be regarded as "noise" or "random variation" and that the game situation constitutes an interaction system which is predictable from the generalized choice theory.

The formal characteristics of the game structure described in Figure 9.3 together with the additional characteristics of Experiment VI are presented in Table 9.3. There were a total of four three-person coalition games run under the conditions of Experiment VI. This meant that there were only four subjects in each player position. Since the structure of the situation was identical for each player, the theory's predictions are identical for each player. Therefore the data from all positions can be pooled. This results in a total N of 12 subjects who are predicted to behave identically and therefore provide a single set of data against which to test the theory.

The experiment described in Table 9.3 was run for only 50 iterations. Pretests of free-interactive games revealed that stabilization occurred fairly rapidly and that is was unnecessary to iterate the game 100 times.

Table 9.3 *Formal Characteristics of Experiment VI*

Player	Payoffs for coalitions with players X and Y	Equity	Sex of subject	Number of subjects
1	2 = $.10 3 = $.05	Low	Male	4
2	1 = $.05 3 = $.10	Low	Male	4
3	1 = $.10 2 = $.05	Low	Male	4

Since the data generated by all subjects in the experiment could be pooled, reporting the general characteristics of the behavior of the interaction system is straightforward. The first points to be considered relate to the probabilities of alternative coalition choices through time and stabilization of choice strategies. Figure 9.4 presents the mean probabilities of five-cent coalition choices through time for subjects in Experiment VI.

The curve reported in Figure 9.4 indicates that subjects stabilize their

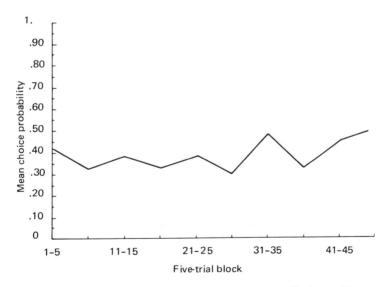

Figure 9.4 *Mean Probability of a Five-Cent Coalition Choice by Players in a Game with Interchangeable Structures.*

choice strategies after an adaptation period of approximately 30 trials. (This period is somewhat longer than had been expected from the pretest results.) Trials 31–50 therefore represent the segment of the experiment within which stable-state choice strategies will be considered to be in evidence and against which the model's predictions will be tested.

Table 9.4 *Mean Stable-State Probabilities of Choices of Five- and 10-Cent Payoff Coalitions for Subjects in Experiment VI*

Coalition	Probability of choosing five- and 10-cent coalitions	Probability of being chosen by five- and 10-cent payoff player
$.10	.5625	.4375
$.05	.4375	.5625

Table 9.4 reports the remainder of the information describing the general characteristics of subject behavior in the game. As indicated in Table 9.4, the mean stable-state probability with which subjects choose the coalition from which they receive a 10-cent payoff is .5625, and the mean probability of a choice of the five-cent coalition is .4375. Note that these probability values define the inputs that each subject receives from the other players in the game as well as his outputs. That is, the mean probability with which a subject is chosen by his 10-cent alternative player is equal to the average probability with which subjects choose their five-cent coalitions. This comes about because each player's five-cent payoff alternative is another player's 10-cent payoff alternative.

Given the estimate for alpha ratios under unequal reward conditions obtained in Section 9.2, it is possible to generate predictions for the behavior of subjects in Experiment VI. Note that *no* data from the free-interactive experiments are used in arriving at these predictions, no data from the free interactive experiments were used in procedures through which the alpha estimate was obtained, and the subjects who participated in the free-interactive experiments were a different set of individuals than those who participated in the robot-interactive experiments. Subjects were, however, drawn from the same population as those who participated in the experiments from which the alpha estimates were obtained. The following is a solution of the equations of the generalized choice model.

The system of simultaneous linear equations presented below is expected to predict the stable-state behavior of the interaction system:

$$4P_{1,2} - \alpha_{1,2}P_{2,1} + \alpha_{1,3}P_{3,1} = 2$$

$$\alpha_{2,1}P_{1,2} - 4P_{2,1} + \alpha_{2,3}P_{3,1} = \alpha_{2,3} - 2$$

$$\alpha_{3,1}P_{1,2} - \alpha_{3,2}P_{2,1} + 4P_{3,1} = \alpha_{3,1} - \alpha_{3,2} + 2$$

Given estimates for the alpha values, these equations can be solved in the usual manner for simultaneous linear equations. For the particular game situation to be predicted at this time, each individual receives five cents from one alternative coalition and 10 cents from the other. Referring to Figure 9.2, it is obvious that $\alpha_{1,2}$, $\alpha_{2,3}$, and $\alpha_{3,1}$ correspond to the utility ratios for coalitions that yield 10 cent payoffs (i.e., $\alpha_{1,2}$ denotes player one's utility ratio for a coalition with player two). Therefore, using the alpha values obtained in Section 9.2,

$$\alpha_{1,2} = \alpha_{2,3} = \alpha_{3,1} = 3.02485$$

Similarly, for the five-cent coalitions,

$$\alpha_{1,3} = \alpha_{2,1} = \alpha_{3,2} = 1.58258$$

Given these values for the alpha ratios, and the appropriate substitutions in the set of equations presented above, it is a straightforward task to solve for the probability with which any player chooses any other player.

Consider, for example, player one. The probability with which he chooses player two can be obtained in the following manner:

$$P_{1,2} = \frac{\begin{vmatrix} 2 & -\alpha_{1,2} & \alpha_{1,3} \\ \alpha_{2,3} - 2 & -4 & \alpha_{2,3} \\ \alpha_{3,1} - \alpha_{3,2} + 2 & -\alpha_{3,2} & 4 \end{vmatrix}}{\begin{vmatrix} 4 & -\alpha_{1,2} & \alpha_{1,3} \\ \alpha_{2,1} & -4 & \alpha_{2,3} \\ \alpha_{3,1} & -\alpha_{3,2} & 4 \end{vmatrix}}$$

$$= \frac{\begin{vmatrix} 2 & -3.02485 & 1.58258 \\ 3.02485 - 2 & -4 & 3.02485 \\ 3.02485 - 1.58258 + 2 & -1.58258 & 4 \end{vmatrix}}{\begin{vmatrix} 4 & -3.02485 & 1.58258 \\ 1.58258 & -4 & 3.02485 \\ 3.02485 & -1.58258 & 4 \end{vmatrix}}$$

$$= \frac{-22.2977}{-38.1954}$$

$$= .5838$$

Given the probability with which player one chooses one of his alternative coalitions, the probability with which he chooses the other coalition will be equal to one minus this value. Therefore:

$$P_{1,2} = .5838$$
$$P_{1,3} = 1 - .5838 = .4162$$

The solution shown above yields predictions for the stable-state probabilities with which player one chooses his 10-cent payoff coalition $(P_{1,2})$ and his five-cent payoff alternative $(P_{1,3})$. Since all players in the game are in interchangeable structural positions, the model yields identical predictions for the probabilities with which each one chooses his 10- and five-cent payoff coalitions. It is unnecessary to show the derivations of predictions for the choice strategies players two and three will adopt. The final predictions for the behavior of the interaction system are given below:

$$P_{1,2} = P_{2,3} = P_{3,1} = .5838$$
$$P_{1,3} = P_{2,1} = P_{3,2} = .4162$$

Table 9.5 reports the results of the application of the theory to the data from Experiment VI. The model yields the prediction that the optimizing choice strategy for all players is to select their five-cent payoff alternative with a probability of .4162 and their 10-cent payoff coalition with a probability of .5838. The choice strategy adopted by subjects was to select their five-cent payoff alternatives with a probability of .4375 and their 10-cent payoff alternatives with a probability of .5625. The absolute difference between the predicted and observed choice strategies was .0213.

Table 9.5   *Results of Application of the Generalized Choice Theory to Data from Experiment VI*

Coalition	Predicted probability of choosing 10- and five-cent payoff coalitions	Observed probability of choosing 10- and five-cent payoff coalitions	|Discrepancy|
$.10	.5838	.5625	
			.0213
$.05	.4162	.4375	

The decision theory was tested in a situation in which an attempt was made to predict more than just the reactions of an individual to a social situation in which the behavior of the other actors was predetermined. The goal was to predict how an individual's utilities for payoffs available from alternative coalitions and his utility for an equitable division of total rewards would influence his decision making, how his behavior would influence the behavior of other members of an interaction system, and how their behaviors would in turn influence his behavior. The problem, then, was to predict the dynamics of a system of freely interacting individuals. Given the formal theory of decision making, estimates of an individual's marginal utility of a payoff and his marginal utility for equity in the distribution of total available rewards, and a formal method for combining predictions for the behavior of each member of an interaction system, it is possible to derive predictions for the behavior of the system that are discrepant from the observed behavior of the system by an absolute value of .02.

9.4 INTERACTION IN GROUPS WITH UNIQUE STRUCTURAL POSITIONS

The second test of the generalized decision theory was conducted in a game situation in which all players occupied structurally unique positions. For reasons of either payoff position differences or the manner in which positions were interconnected, or both, it was necessary to treat each player in the game as being affected by different values of the theoretical variables and therefore as providing a unique data point. Multiple observations of behavior in a given player position were obtained by replicating identical games with different subjects. Data were pooled from subjects who participated in different games but who occupied the same structural positions in their respective games.

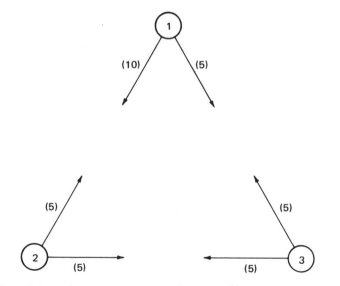

Figure 9.5 *A Coalition Game with Unique Structural Positions.* The notation should be read as follows: Ⓧ defines a player; Ⓧ_(5)_→ defines the payoff that player *X* receives for a coalition with the player indicated by the directed line.

The game represented in Figure 9.5 was selected as the concrete setting within which to conduct the research. It was chosen because it was believed to be one of the more interesting and less intuitively obvious of the games with which the estimated alpha ratios permitted research to be conducted. The game was one in which player one occupied a 5-10 payoff position and both players two and three were in 5-5 positions. The three players were interconnected so that a coalition with player two was a 10-cent alternative for player one and a coalition with player three was a five-cent coalition alternative for both players one and two. The game structure was one in which only player one had a clear monetary preference between his alternative coalitions. Players two and three were offered five cents for forming either of their possible coalitions and therefore were, on strict economic grounds, indifferent between alternative coalitions.

The factors that were predicted to influence the behavior of the individuals with whom a player was in interaction introduced some interesting considerations. For example, although players two and three were in equivalent payoff positions (5-5), they were in interaction with individuals who had quite different motivations to form coalitions with them. Player two was in interaction with players one and three. Player three was in interaction with players one and two.

For player two the motivations of his potential partners to ally with him were as follows. Since a coalition with player two yielded a 10-cent payoff for player one and his alternative coalition paid only five cents, he would be quite anxious to form an alliance with player two. Player three was paid five cents for forming either of his alternative coalitions, and he would be equally interested in either possible coalition.

For player three the situation was one in which no other player was greatly motivated to form coalitions with him. A coalition with player three yielded only five cents for player one. This was only one-half of the amount that he was paid for a coalition with player two. Player two was paid five cents for forming any coalition and therefore was no more interested in a coalition with player three than he was in a coalition with player one. Indifference was the strongest economic motivation for either of his potential partners to form coalitions with player three.

Each player's equity considerations added to the complexity of the game structure. Consider player two, for example. He is in the best position to form a permanent alliance with either of the others since he represents player one's preferred alternative, and player three will be oriented to choose him since his other potential partner (player one) will not be greatly interested in forming coalitions with him. If player two has no concern about the welfare of the other individuals in the game, he will permit a permanent alliance to form with one of his possible coalition partners. This is, of course, highly detrimental to the excluded individual. If, as the theory predicts, player two is concerned about the welfare of the other players in the game, he will attempt to bring about conditions that equalize the number of coalitions that they are each able to enter. It is even conceivable that player two can arrange matters so that he will still be included in a coalition on every trial. Assume that player two has entered into a temporary alliance with one of the other players. Given the structure of the game, the excluded player will attempt to break the alliance by making consistent choices of player two. Player two is therefore put in a position in which, in order to include both of the other players in a more nearly equal number of coalitions, he must alternate in some manner between player one and player three. This strategy, however, involves some monetary risks for player two since it is possible that through imperfect coordination no coalition will form on some trials or that the other two players will enter into an alliance to his detriment.

Due to all of the above considerations, the game structure selected as the setting in which to conduct the research is considered to be a complex social situation in which each of the participants of the interaction system is faced with a decision problem that, for a number of reasons, is different from the decision problems faced by the other participants of the system. The test of the theory is its ability to predict the decision making of each player in the game and, therefore, the behavior of the system of interacting individuals.

The conditions under which Experiment VII was conducted were identical to the conditions of Experiment VI except for the number of iterations of the game and the payoffs available to the players for alternative coalitions. Table 9.6 reports the formal characteristics of the experiment. Since in

Table 9.6 *Formal Characteristics of Experiment VII*

Player	Payoffs for coalitions with players X and Y	Equity	Sex of subject	Number of subjects
1	2 = $.10 3 = $.05	Low	Male	14
2	1 = $.05 3 = $.05	Low	Male	14
3	1 = $.05 2 = $.05	Low	Male	14

Experiment VI it took a somewhat longer period of time for subjects to stabilize their choice strategies than pretests had indicated it would require, it was decided to lengthen Experiment VII. The length of the experiment was increased by 20% and the game was iterated for 60 trials. There were a total of 14 games conducted for the experiment. This meant that there were 42 participants in the experiment with 14 subjects in each of the unique player positions.

The first aspect of the data from Experiment VII to be considered concerns the process characteristics of the behavior of subjects in the three player positions. The data generated by subjects in each of the three positions will be examined separately. Figure 9.6 reports the process data for subjects in

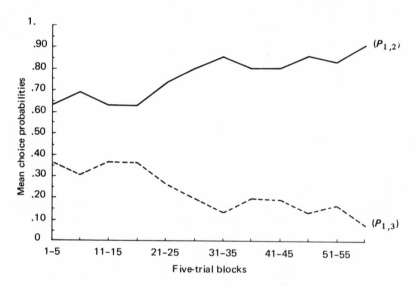

Figure 9.6 *Mean Probabilities of Player One's Choices Through Time.*

the player one position. The mean probabilities of choices of players two and three are presented for blocks of five trials. Since the probability of player one's choosing player two ($P_{1,2}$) equals one minus the probability of his choosing player three ($P_{1,2} = 1 - P_{1,3}$), the two curves presented in Figure 9.6 are redundant. The reason for reporting both curves is to simply make easier the task of communicating the results of the research.

The trend in the distribution of choices by subjects in the player one position is quite clear. As the theory predicts, subjects are initially oriented toward selection of player two as a coalition partner and this preference becomes more definite as the experiment continues. After approximately 25 trials, subjects appear to stabilize their choice strategies at a level that remains constant for the duration of the experiment. Calculation of the stable-state choice strategy for subjects in the player one position was therefore based upon the last 35 iterations of the game (trials 26 through 60).

The process data for subjects in the player two position are presented in

Figure 9.7. The theory predicts that subjects in this position will initially be indifferent between alternative coalitions since each coalition yields five cents every time it is formed. The theory also generates the prediction that the probabilities with which the subjects are chosen by players one and three will cause them to modify their distribution of choices of these players. Observe that for the first 20 repetitions of the game subjects in the player two position distribute choices between players one and three with nearly equal probabilities. The mean probabilities of choices of alternative coalitions become clearly differentiated in the fifth trial block (trials 21–26) and remain constant throughout the duration of the experiment. Subjects in the player two position are treated as having stabilized their choice strategies for the last 40 iterations of the game (trials 21 through 60).

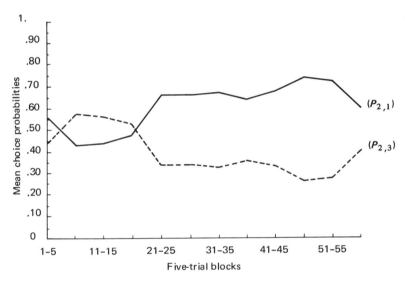

Figure 9.7 *Mean Probabilities of Player Two's Choices Through Time.*

The data reported in Figure 9.8 are for the mean probabilities of choices of players one and two by player number three. Subjects in this position are predicted to be initially indifferent between alternative coalitions and to alter their behavior as a function of the probabilities with which they are chosen by each of the other individuals in their game. As shown in Figure 9.8, players in position number three require about 20 trials to stabilize their choice strategies. (Note that relative to subjects in the number two position, position three subjects demonstrate a more consistent early difference in the probabilities with which they choose their alternative possible coalitions. It will be

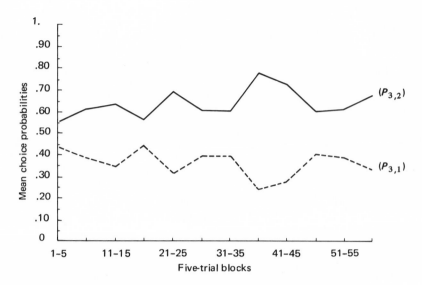

Figure 9.8 *Mean Probabilities of Player Three's Choices Through Time.*

shown below that this differentiation comes about as a function of the different behaviors of the individuals with whom players two and three are in interaction.) Based on inspection of this data, it is reasonable to identify the last 40 iterations of the game as the segment of the experiment within which subjects in position three are in stable state.

Table 9.7 presents the mean stable-state probabilities with which subjects

Table 9.7 *Mean Stable-State Probabilities of Choices of Alternative Coalitions for Subjects in Experiment VII*

Player	Probability of choosing players X and Y*	Probabilities of being chosen by players X and Y
1	$P_{1,2} = .8388$	$P_{2,1} = .6714$
	$P_{1,3} = .1612$	$P_{3,1} = .3393$
2	$P_{2,1} = .6714$	$P_{1,2} = .8388$
	$P_{2,3} = .3286$	$P_{3,2} = .6607$
3	$P_{3,1} = .3393$	$P_{1,3} = .1612$
	$P_{3,2} = .6607$	$P_{2,3} = .3286$

*The notation $P_{x,y}$ is to be read as the probability with which player X chooses player Y.

in each of the three player positions distribute their choices of alternative possible coalitions. When properly viewed, the entries in Table 9.7 describe all of the behavior of the three-person interaction system. The entries in the first column specify the stable-state choice strategies of the three players. These may be regarded as each player's outputs to the other system members. The entries in the second column are organized in terms of each player's inputs from the other participants in the system. For example, player one is chosen by player two with a probability of .6714 ($P_{2,1} = .6714$). Player one's output to player two ($P_{1,2}$) is a selection of player two with a probability of .8388. Although it is convenient to discuss the interactions in the game in terms of inputs and outputs, it should be remembered that the mechanical imagery evoked by these terms is an oversimplification of the action of the system. Player X's choice strategy is a cause of the outputs of players Y and Z, and players Y and Z's outputs affect player X's strategy. The values reported in Table 9.6 represent the interaction system in a state of equilibrium that is dependent upon each member's maintenance of a stable choice strategy.

The dynamic characteristics of the interaction system may be more clearly viewed through presentation of the process data in a modified form. The presentation of subjects' mean stable-state choice strategies in Table 9.7 casts the data in terms of the inputs and outputs of each member of the system. The graphs reporting the process aspects of the experiments can be modified in order to demonstrate interactive aspects of the data in the same fashion. Figure 9.9 presents a process-oriented representation of player one's inputs

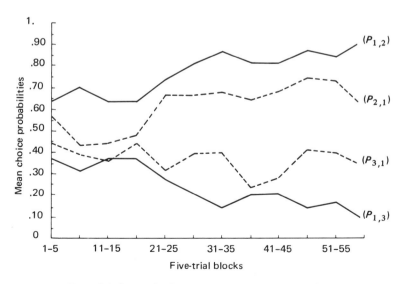

Figure 9.9 *Player One's Inputs and Outputs Through Time.*

and outputs. The four curves presented in Figure 9.9 report the probabilities with which player one is chosen by each of the other players and the probabilities with which he chooses each of the two individuals with whom he is in interaction. Observe that throughout the experiment players in the number one position choose player two (the 10-cent coalition) with a greater probability than that with which they are chosen by player two. This result is expected since for player one the relative value of a 1-2 coalition is much greater than it is for player two.

In terms of the theory's predictions for behavior in interactive situations, it is important to note the degree to which input and output curves parallel one another. (This is particularly true for player one's outputs to and inputs from player two.) Although the decision theory predicts average stable-state values for choice strategies, any dynamic formulation that was consistent with its axioms would have to predict co-variation in input and output values. The fact that such co-variation is evident in Figure 9.9 is quite important.

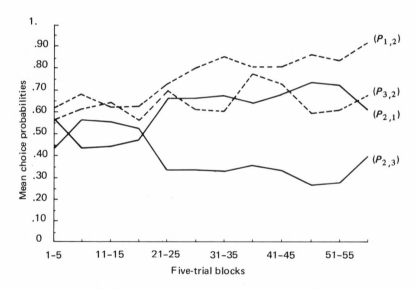

Figure 9.10 *Player Two's Inputs and Outputs Through Time.*

Figure 9.10 reports the process data for player two. The situation in this case is quite different from that facing player one. Both players one and three are clearly engaged in competition for alliances with player two. It has already been argued that player two's initial indifference between alternative coalitions is accounted for by his payoff position (he gets five cents for either coalition). Observe that during the prestabilization period (trials one through 20), player two exhibits a preference for player three over player one. This relative preference is in evidence despite the fact that players in the number one position select player two with a slightly higher average probability than do players in the number three position. As subjects move into stable state, the differentiation between the choice strategies of players one and three becomes more pronounced and players in the number one position choose player two with a substantially higher probability than do individuals in the number three position. Player two responds by adjusting his outputs to the new set of inputs from the other members of the system.

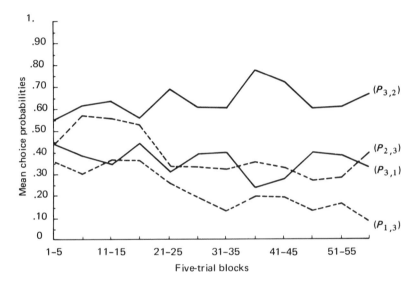

Figure 9.11 *Player Three's Inputs and Outputs Through Time.*

The process data indicate that the stable-state choice strategy adopted by player two (greater selection of player one than player three) is explained by the difference in the probabilities with which he is chosen by the two other members of the system. It cannot be accounted for by player two's payoff position, since his payoffs for alternative coalitions are equal. Also note that player two tends to choose player one less frequently than player one chooses him. It would seem reasonable to attribute this underselection to an attempt to maintain a more equitable division of rewards among players.

The input and output process data for player three are presented in Figure 9.11. It can be seen from these curves that player three's choice strategy reflects the relative probabilities with which he is chosen by the other players in the game. Throughout the entire course of the experiment, player two chooses player three with a higher probability than does player one, and player three responds with a consistent preference for player two in his distribution of choices. It is interesting to note that once the interaction system reaches stabilization (starting at approximately trial 20), the curves reporting player three's choice of player two ($P_{3,2}$) and player two's choices of player three ($P_{2,3}$) show some degree of co-variation. There is little evidence of co-variation between curves for the probabilities with which player one chooses player three ($P_{1,3}$) and player three chooses player one ($P_{3,1}$).

The analysis of the inputs to players and their outputs through time indicates a number of things about interaction in the game. It is clear that players in the game are as sensitive to variations in the behaviors of the individuals with whom they are actually in interaction as were subjects in the robot-interactive experiments to variations in the behaviors of the robot players. This is particularly interesting since the probabilities reported in Figures 9.9, 9.10, and 9.11 are calculated for blocks of only five trials. Even with this small number of trials, there are numerous points at which two curves show concomitant variation. That is, as player X changes the probability with which he chooses player Y, player Y modifies the probability with which he chooses player X. The fact that concomitant variation of the curves can be observed with the block length used to calculate the points for the curves reported in these figures indicates that modification takes place in a very short period of time (less than five iterations of the game).

It is, of course, impossible to definitely determine from the existing data which player initiates the change in his choice strategy and which player modifies his behavior as a reaction to the change. The pattern with which pairs of players co-vary their choices does, however, suggest a possible explanation for pair-wise interactions demonstrated by co-variation in Figures 9.9, 9.10, and 9.11. The data suggest that player two exercises the greatest degree of control in short-run variations in behavior. It has already been noted that any player can affect the equilibrium point of the system by adopting a fixed strategy and refusing to modify his behavior in response to the behaviors of the other participants in the interaction. If it is assumed that all players move toward a maximizing strategy as, it will be shown, do the players in Experiment VII, there is still a question as to whether or not all players have equal power to affect the interaction system in terms of variations around the equilibrium point. Both players one and three demonstrate co-variation in behavior with player two. Although alternative explanations might be proposed, it seems reasonable to suggest that since players one and three are in competition for alliances with player two, player two exercises relatively greater control over the others' behaviors than they do over his. Player two has considerable reward power over the other participants in the game. Slight changes in his choice strategy seem to produce substantial changes in the behaviors of the other players.

The choice theory does not directly address the question of control in the sense that it is used here, and hence it would not be expected to yield predictions for relative control for players in the game. In terms of general interaction problems under consideration, it should be noted that the control variable accounts only for variation around the major decision strategy predicted by the theory. In order to predict the more general decision strategy, it does not seem necessary to consider the question of relative control.

The characteristics of the game structure have been discussed and the general tendencies in the behavior of players in each of the unique structural positions have been analyzed. It therefore seems appropriate at this point to directly address the problem of testing the theory's power to predict the dynamics of three-person interaction systems. Since each member of the system occupies a unique position, it will be necessary to separately derive predictions for the behavior of subjects in each of the three player positions. The first of the model's predictions will be generated for the behavior of subjects in the player one position.

Predictions for player one's choice strategy are arrived at by introducing appropriate alpha values and by solving the system of linear equations that describe the interaction system. The system of linear equations is:

$$4P_{1,2} - \alpha_{1,2}P_{2,1} + \alpha_{1,3}P_{3,1} = 2$$
$$\alpha_{2,1}P_{1,2} - 4P_{2,1} + \alpha_{2,3}P_{3,1} = \alpha_{2,3} - 2$$
$$\alpha_{3,1}P_{1,2} - \alpha_{3,2}P_{2,1} + 4P_{3,1} = \alpha_{3,1} - \alpha_{3,2} + 2$$

The alpha ratios that will be introduced were obtained in Section 9.2. Inspection of Figure 9.5 reveals that player one is in an unequal alpha situation in which he receives 10 cents for a coalition with player two and five cents for a coalition with player three. Therefore:

$$\alpha_{1,2} = 3.02485$$
$$\alpha_{1,3} = 1.58258$$

Players two and three are in equal alpha situations since they receive five cents for either of their possible coalitions. Therefore:

$$\alpha_{2,1} = \alpha_{2,3} = \alpha_{3,1} = \alpha_{3,2} = 3.49663$$

Using these alpha values the model predicts that the choice strategy maximizing player one's expected utility is to choose players two and three with the following probabilities:

$$P_{1,2} = \frac{\begin{vmatrix} 2 & -\alpha_{1,2} & \alpha_{1,3} \\ \alpha_{2,3} - 2 & -4 & \alpha_{2,3} \\ \alpha_{3,1} - \alpha_{3,2} + 2 & -\alpha_{3,2} & 4 \end{vmatrix}}{\begin{vmatrix} 4 & -\alpha_{1,2} & \alpha_{1,3} \\ \alpha_{2,1} & -4 & \alpha_{2,3} \\ \alpha_{3,1} & -\alpha_{3,2} & 4 \end{vmatrix}}$$

$$= \frac{\begin{vmatrix} 2 & -3.02485 & 1.58258 \\ 3.49663 - 2 & -4 & 3.49663 \\ 3.49663 - 3.49663 + 2 & -3.49663 & 4 \end{vmatrix}}{\begin{vmatrix} 4 & -3.02485 & 1.58258 \\ 3.49663 & -4 & 3.49663 \\ 3.49663 & -3.49663 & 4 \end{vmatrix}}$$

$$= \frac{-6.21366}{-6.98479}$$

$$= .8896$$

$$P_{1,3} = 1 - P_{1,2} = .1104$$

For player two the model yields a maximizing choice strategy with the following values:

$$P_{2,1} = \frac{\begin{vmatrix} 4 & 2 & \alpha_{1,3} \\ \alpha_{2,1} & \alpha_{2,3} - 2 & \alpha_{2,3} \\ \alpha_{3,1} & \alpha_{3,1} - \alpha_{3,2} + 2 & 4 \end{vmatrix}}{\begin{vmatrix} 4 & -\alpha_{1,2} & \alpha_{1,3} \\ \alpha_{2,1} & -4 & \alpha_{2,3} \\ \alpha_{3,1} & -\alpha_{3,2} & 4 \end{vmatrix}}$$

$$= \frac{\begin{vmatrix} 4 & 2 & 1.58258 \\ 3.49663 & 3.49663 - 2 & 3.49663 \\ 3.49663 & 3.49663 - 3.49663 + 2 & 4 \end{vmatrix}}{\begin{vmatrix} 4 & 3.02485 & 1.58258 \\ 3.49663 & -4 & 3.49663 \\ 3.49663 & -3.49663 & 4 \end{vmatrix}}$$

$$= \frac{-4.76166}{-6.98479}$$

$$= .6817$$

$$P_{2,3} = 1 - P_{2,1} = .3183$$

Using the alpha values specified previously, the model's prediction for player three's maximizing choice strategy is:

$$P_{3,1} = \frac{\begin{vmatrix} 4 & -\alpha_{1,2} & 2 \\ \alpha_{2,1} & -4 & \alpha_{2,3} - 2 \\ \alpha_{3,1} & -\alpha_{3,2} & \alpha_{3,1} - \alpha_{3,2} + 2 \end{vmatrix}}{\begin{vmatrix} 4 & -\alpha_{1,2} & \alpha_{1,3} \\ \alpha_{2,1} & -4 & \alpha_{2,3} \\ \alpha_{3,1} & -\alpha_{3,2} & 4 \end{vmatrix}}$$

$$= \frac{\begin{vmatrix} 4 & -3.02485 & 2 \\ 3.49663 & -4 & 3.49663 - 2 \\ 3.49663 & -3.49663 & 3.49663 - 3.49663 + 2 \end{vmatrix}}{\begin{vmatrix} 4 & -3.02485 & 1.58258 \\ 3.49663 & -4 & 3.49663 \\ 3.49663 & -3.49663 & 4 \end{vmatrix}}$$

$$= \frac{-2.22313}{-6.98479}$$

$$= .3183$$

$$P_{3,2} = 1 - P_{3,1} = .6817 [4]$$

Table 9.8 summarizes the model's predictions for the behavior of each participant in the interaction system and reports the observed stable-state choice strategies for subjects in each of the three player positions. The model predicts that for subjects in the player one position the maximizing choice strategy is to choose player two with a probability of .8896 and player three with a probability of .1104. Subjects in position number one choose player two with a probability of .8388 and player three with a probability of .1612. The absolute discrepancy between the predicted and observed choice strategies is .0508. For subjects in the player two position the maximizing choice strategy is a .6817 probability of a player one choice and a .3183 probability of a player three choice. The observed strategy ($P_{2,1} = .6714$ and $P_{2,3} = .3286$) is discrepant from the predicted strategy by an absolute value of .0103. For subjects in the player three position, the strategy that maximizes expected utility is to choose player one with a probability of .3183 and player two with a probability of .6817. The observed choice strategy of

---

4. Note the similarity in predictions for the maximizing behaviors of players two and three. The model predicts that each will distribute his choices with probabilities of .6817 and .3183. Player two is predicted to choose player one with the greater probability, and player three is predicted to choose player one with the lesser of the two probabilities. The similarity in the values of these probabilities is accidental. The model does not always predict identical strategies for players in identical payoff positions. For example, if player one's maximizing strategy was a selection of player two with a probability of .9255 and player three with a probability of .0745, the model's predictions for players two and three's maximizing strategies would be $P_{2,1} = .7392$ and $P_{2,3} = .2608$, and $P_{3,1} = .3411$ and $P_{3,2} = .6589$.

$P_{3,1} = .3393$ and $P_{3,2} = .6607$ is discrepant from the maximizing strategy by $|.0210|$.

The power of the model to predict the dynamics of the interaction system is obviously considerable. The model argues that all members of the system

Table 9.8 *Results of Application of the Generalized Choice Theory to Data from Experiment VII*

Player position	Predicted choice strategy	Observed choice strategy	|Discrepancy|
1	$P_{1,2} = .8896$	.8388	
			.0508
	$P_{1,3} = .1104$	.1612	
2	$P_{2,1} = .6817$	.6714	
			.0103
	$P_{2,3} = .3183$	.3286	
3	$P_{3,1} = .3183$	.3393	
			.0210
	$P_{3,2} = .6817$	.6607	

may be treated as if they are acting so as to maximize expected utility in their decision making, that each player will adopt a stable choice strategy, and consequently that the interaction system will arrive at an equilibrium point. In addition, the model predicts the precise maximizing strategy that each player will adopt, and consequently it specifies the equilibrium point to which the system will move. The test of the generalization of the theory to the behavior of interaction systems is the accuracy with which it is able to predict the values of the stable-state strategies of each member of the system. The average absolute discrepancy between the theory's predictions for the subjects' maximizing strategies and their observed strategies was .0274. The greatest discrepancy was only $|.0508|$, and the smallest was $|.0103|$.

9.5 SUMMARY

In this chapter a generalized version of the choice theory was tested by comparing its predictions to the observed equilibrium behavior of two interaction systems. The generalization of the theory rests on the assumption that individuals act so as to maximize utility in their decision making. Given the viability of this basic assumption, the other substantive axioms of the theory, and the model that formalizes the postulated relationships, it should be possible to predict the dynamics of interactive behavior.

The model was subjected to two independent tests, with predictions generated for the equilibrium point for two different interaction systems. In one of the interaction systems, subjects occupied positions that were theoretically interchangeable, and all participants were predicted to adopt the same stable-state behavior. In the second research setting, all subjects occupied positions that were theoretically unique, and players were predicted to adopt different stable-state choice strategies. The results of the two tests are summarized in Figures 9.12 and 9.13.

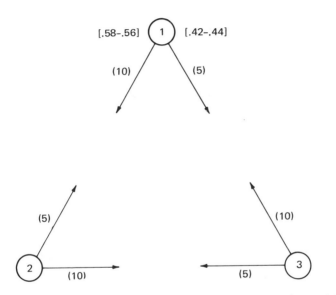

Figure 9.12 *Predicted and Observed System Behavior in a Game with Interchangeable Structural Positions.* The notation should be read as follows: ⊗ defines a player; ⊗___(5)___→ defines the payoff that player *X* receives for a coalition with the player indicated by the directed line; [.58-.56] are the predicted maximizing choice probability and the observed probability with which the player makes the indicated choice.

The graph in Figure 9.12 represents the structure of the first coalition game to which the theory was applied. In this game, each player was offered 10 cents for one coalition and five cents for the other. Players were interconnected so that each player's 10-cent coalition was another player's five-cent alternative. The figures in brackets are the predicted and observed choice probabilities for participants in the game. The entry for the subjects' choices of the 10-cent alternative [.58—.56], is read as follows: The predicted maximizing strategy is to select the 10-cent alternative with a probability of .58, and the observed probability with which subjects chose this alternative is .56. Since all players in the system occupy identical structural positions, the equilibrium point for the system is for each player to distribute his choices with these probabilities. The absolute discrepancy between the observed and predicted equilibrium point for the system is .02 in the probabilities of events.

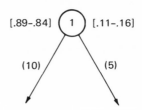

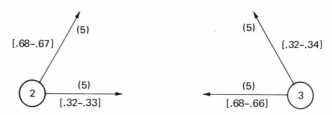

Figure 9.13 *Predicted and Observed Behavior in a Game with Unique Structural Positions.* The notation should be read as follows: ⊗ defines a player; ⊗__(5)__→ defines the payoff that player *X* receives for a coalition with the player indicated by the directed line; [.89-.84] are the predicted maximizing choice probability and the observed probability with which the player makes the indicated choice.

The coalition game represented in Figure 9.13 served as the research setting for the second application of the theory. In this game all players occupied structurally unique positions. The theory was therefore used to generate predictions for the behavior of players in each position. The predictions for optimizing strategies and observed choice probabilities are entered in the same manner as they were for Figure 9.12. Inspection of these entries indicates that the model's predictions are quite close to the choice strategies adopted by players. The average absolute discrepancy between the predicted equilibrium of the system and the observed equilibrium point is .03.

10

Some Differences Between Research Programs

Since the goal of the present research was to test an extension of the scope of the general decision-making theory and the optimal conditions under which to conduct the investigation necessitated departures from the procedures used by Siegel in his research on nonsocial decision making, direct comparisons between research programs are not usually possible. Direct comparisons between programs are, however, relatively less informative than comparisons of the theory's power to predict behavior under sets of theoretically similar, although concretely different, situations. Comparisons of this type were drawn in the conclusions of appropriate chapters of the report and need not be repeated here.

There are a number of specific differences between the research program on nonsocial decision making and the program reported here that have significance with regard to theoretical issues and therefore will be considered. In some cases, procedural differences were introduced in order to systematically vary procedures from those employed by Siegel, and in other cases, the differences were necessitated by the requirements of the coalition game setting. In the conclusion to the *Choice, Strategy and Utility* monograph, a number of points to which future research should be addressed were noted. These points dealt with either procedural issues that affected scope considerations or basic theoretical questions. The research reported herein was relevant to a number of these issues.

In the nonsocial decision-making experiments all subjects were male. Siegel points out that:

> While we would scarcely assert that only men may be expected to maximize expected utility in a repetitive-choice situation or that the particular utility function postulated by the model is sex-specific, we must note that to date our findings are derived from males (p. 147).

In the social decision-making research, samples of both male and female subjects were obtained for Experiments I, II, and III. This permitted the choice theory to be tested with populations of both sexes and direct comparisons to be made between the behavior of males and females under identical experimental conditions. There were sufficient data to test the theory for both sexes under equal alpha experimental conditions. A comparison of the results of these applications of the model is presented in Table 10.1. Clearly, in both applications, predictions for the behavior of male subjects are more accurate than predictions for the behavior of female subjects. The differential accuracy is, however, more likely a function of the sample sizes employed for measurement and prediction than it is a function of sex-related differences in behavior. It is the case with all the research testing the choice theory that the greater the sample size the more accurate the model's predictions. The sample sizes for male subjects were on the average nearly three times the size of those for female subjects. The important aspect of the comparison is that the model predicts rather well for both males and females.

Given that the model predicts with considerable accuracy for male and female subjects, there is a second point that should be considered. The question concerns the assignment of utility to monetary payoffs and equity. Is there any evidence that males and females operate with different utility ratios? For example, if, relative to female subjects, males assigned a greater utility to the monetary payoffs offered for forming coalitions, and the same utility to equity, it would be expected that they would adopt choice strategies closer to a pure monetary maximizing, (1-0), distribution. Under equal alpha experimental conditions, the strategy that maximized monetary gain was to predict the more frequent event with probability one. With the π values employed in the unequal alpha condition (Condition C), the monetary maximizing strategy was also to predict the more frequent event with probability one. If there were any gross, sex-related differences in utility ratios they would result in different mean choice strategies for samples of male and female subjects. The data reported in Table 10.2 reveal that the average

Table 10.1 Comparison of Accuracy of Prediction with Male and Female Subjects under Equal Alpha Conditions*

Treatment condition	Sex	π_1	π_2	$a_1 = a_2$	N	Predicted P_1 and P_2	Observed P_1 and P_2	|Discrepancy|
A	Male	.70	.30	$.05	22	.8500	.8495	.0005
						.1500	.1505	
A'	Female	.70	.30	$.05	6	.9500	.9375	.0125
						.0500	.0625	
B	Male	.60	.40	$.05	21	.6747	.6750	.0003
						.3253	.3250	
B'	Female	.60	.40	$.05	9	.7188	.7250	.0062
						.2812	.2750	

*Stabilization points were selected on the basis of inspection of the data.

131

choice strategies adopted by male and female subjects are quite similar. If comparisons are made between the distributions of the number of alternative one choices per subject for samples of male and female subjects, no statistically significant differences between samples are found (Mann Whitney U, two-tailed at $P < .05$).

Table 10.2 *Comparison of Choice Behavior of Males and Females*

Treatment condition	Mean P_1 and P_2		Monetary maximizing pure strategy
	Males	Females	
A*	P_1 = .8100	.8433	P_1 = 1
	P_2 = .1900	.1567	P_2 = 0
B	P_1 = .6162	.6899	P_1 = 1
	P_2 = .3832	.3111	P_2 = 0
C	P_1 = .4971	.4669	P_1 = 1
	P_2 = .5029	.5338	P_2 = 0
D	P_1 = .6391	.5817	P_1 = 1
	P_2 = .3609	.4183	P_2 = 0

*Conditions *A*, *B*, and *C* were conducted with a low equity manipulation. A high equity manipulation was used in condition *D*.

It is interesting to note that female subjects show no indication of a greater concern for equity than do males when all subjects are exposed to the same set of experimental instructions. Vinacke has claimed that females playing the coalition game "are less concerned with winning, as such, and more concerned with arriving at a fair and friendly solution to the problem. The task for them is to determine a way in which no one suffers" (Vinacke, 1959b, p. 357). The data generated in the present research do not support this contention. In fact, as Caplow has noted, Vinacke's conclusion "is heavily dependent upon statistical differences that are not significant" (Caplow, 1968, p. 31). Vinacke has also suggested that females have a tendency to form coalitions when none are necessary (Vinacke, 1959b). Caplow proposed that this conclusion is consistent with "the experimenters' preconceived notion of pliant, accommodating females and brutally competitive males," but that "lacking the impression gained from direct observation, I cannot discern in Vinacke's meticulous tables the difference in strategic style between sexes that he claims to have found" (Caplow, 1968, p. 32).

Even if the question of statistical significance is disregarded and only the pattern of results is considered in the researches reported here, there is still no reason to accept Vinacke's conclusion concerning sex-related differences. Of the three treatments in which a low-equity manipulation was employed (*A*, *B*, and *C*), two resulted in females adopting a more nearly pure economically maximizing strategy. In the one case in which a high-equity manipulation was employed, the females exhibited a more nearly equal division of selections of robot players. Therefore, in half of the cases females demonstrated a greater tendency to adopt the more "brutally competitive" strategy.

Additional data on the question of sex-related differences in competitive strategies are reported by Rapoport and Chammah (1965). When comparisons are made between the behaviors of pairs of males, pairs of females, and mixed pairs playing the prisoner's dilemma game, the results are that the pairs of males display the greatest propensity to cooperate, mixed pairs are second, and pairs of females show the greatest propensity to make noncooperative choices. When the behavior of subjects in male-female pairs is examined, it is the female member who tends to exploit the male.

The data on sex-related differences in competitive behavior are sufficiently vague that it seems prudent to allow discretion to be the better part of valor and to refrain from attempting to offer any conclusion. Since the question to be decided is whether females display greater competitive tendencies than do males, or whether there are no sex-related differences, rather than whether males adopt more competitive strategies than do females, one thing seems certain. Vinacke's conclusion regarding sex-related differences is untenable.

The procedures employed by Siegel were designed to convince subjects that the behavior of the light bulbs was fixed prior to the start of the experiment and would not be altered during the session. Although this was the true state of affairs, some subjects tended to doubt the veracity of the experimenter's statements and believed that he was altering the sequence of illuminations depending on how the subject chose. In order to reduce suspicion, the later experiments in the series were automated, and subjects were shown the paper tape on which the behaviors of the bulbs were programmed. Since in the social decision-making experiments subjects were led to believe that they were interacting with two other individuals, there was no question of their operating with the cognition that the events they were to predict were determined prior to the start of the experiment. Clearly, subjects in the coalition game studies believed that the future behavior of the robots was contingent on their actions. Since the model predicted adequately under these circumstances, it appears that it is unnecessary to restrict application of the theory to situations in which subjects believe there is no interaction between their behaviors and the future behavior of the events they are trying to predict. The successful utilization of the theory in free interactive situations demonstrates that it is unnecessary to restrict its application to situations of only perceived interaction and that it may be used in order to conceptualize behavior in situations in which the subject's behavior has a true effect on future states of nature.

It is interesting to note that while the change from a believed noninteractive situation (the Siegel experiments) to a believed interactive setting (the robot-interactive coalition games) has no effects on the predictive power of the theory, it substantially affects certain characteristics of behavior. In Chapter 7 it was shown that subjects adapt to the probability structure of the experiment much more rapidly when they operate under believed interactive conditions (see pp. 61 to 64). The explanation for why this should occur is by no means immediately apparent. Unfortunately, since there were changes in two potentially causal variables, it is not possible to determine why there was such a great change in the rates at which subjects modified their behaviors. The change from the light-guessing experiments to the coalition game experiments entailed changes in both the subjects' beliefs about the nature of the cause of the events that they were to predict and a change in their beliefs about contingency.

In the light-guessing experiments, subjects were instructed that the sequence they were to predict was determined in advance and that it was unalterable and therefore independent of their behaviors. Subjects were operating in an environment that would likely have been perceived as being impersonal and in which the sequence of light bulb illuminations would have been perceived as being random or, at most, patterned in some mechanical fashion. In the coalition game researches, the believed causes of the sequence of choices with which subjects were confronted were two other players. Supposedly, their future behaviors could be modified by the actions of the subject. It seems reasonable to consider whether greater sensitivity to the sequence of events comes about due to changes in subjects' perceptions of the nature of the generating agent of the sequence, changes in the possibilities for affecting future states of nature, or only when both changes are present. Modification of the procedures for the light-guessing experiment and the coalition game researches could easily be made in order to isolate the cause of the substantial change in the rate at which subjects adapt to the probability structure of their environments.

Siegel noted that due to practical difficulties it was not possible to conduct any experiments in which subjects served as their own controls. It was suggested, however, that:

> Since the utility parameters in the model are subject-based as well as condition-based, a rich and powerful test of the model would be provided by an experiment in which the utility parameters were estimated for a group of subjects under one condition and then used to predict the choice behavior of the same subjects under another condition (p. 155).

Since subjects in the coalition game researches adapted to the probability structure of the environment in a relatively short period of time, it was possible to perform an experiment in which subjects served as their own controls. The experiment is reported in detail in Chapter 7 (pp. 71–77). In addition to being able to demonstrate through this procedure that group means can be accurately predicted when measurements are taken on a single group and used to predict that group's behavior under changed experimental conditions, it was possible to consider the model's power to predict an individual's behavior. Although only 40 trials were used as the basis on which to measure each subject's particular utility assignments, and predictions were compared against his decisions on a subsequent 40 iterations, the model's predictions are reasonably accurate (see Table 7.14). The important point is that the theory proves to be consistent and fairly accurate when applied to the behavior of single individuals even under minimally satisfactory conditions.

In all of the light-guessing experiments in which the π values summed to one the restriction was enforced that the events be mutually exclusive with regard to occurrence on a given trial. If π_1 equaled .70 and π_2 was set at .30, the sequence of events was determined such that in each block of 10 trials bulb one would illuminate seven times and bulb two would illuminate on three occasions. On no trials would both bulbs illuminate, and on no trial would neither bulb illuminate. Although the formal structure of the model permits the occurrence of events to be independently determined, the Siegel researches did not yield tests of the theory under this condition. In the coalition game experiments, the character of the research situation required that the events occur independently of one another. The mutual exclusion condition was relaxed, and on some trials the subject was selected by both robots and on some trials he was selected by neither. The results of the coalition game researches, in both the robot- and free-interactive games, indicate that relaxing the mutual exclusion condition does not affect the power of the model.

The final major point on which Siegel suggested that research should be conducted and which was addressed in the coalition game experiments concerns the assignment of payoffs to events under unequal alpha conditions. In the unequal alpha light-guessing experiments, the highest payoff was always associated with the more frequent event. Under these circumstances, subjects were oriented toward making most of their choices of the event that was both most frequent and most rewarding. The more complex decision problem, high payoff for predicting infrequent events, was never empirically treated. In the coalition game researches three unequal alpha treatment conditions were run. In all conditions the larger payoff, 10 cents, was associated with the less frequent event and the smaller payoff, five cents, was associated with the more likely event. The event parameters in the three treatment conditions were .80 and .20, .70 and .30, and .60 and .40. The results of application of the model to the data generated in these treatment conditions are reported in Chapter 8 and reveal that assignment of payoffs to events in the more complex manner does not affect the model's accuracy.

The points discussed in this chapter were raised since they represent issues of relevance to the general decision-making theory and issues on which the experimental program conducted by Siegel and his associates differed from the researches in the context of the coalition game. Several of the restrictive assumptions under which the light-guessing experiments were run were relaxed in the coalition game studies and did not adversely affect the model's predictive power.

11

Applications of the Theory to Additional Interaction Systems

It has been shown that the formal decision theory can be generalized in order to predict the dynamics of systems of freely interacting individuals in a specified social context. In this chapter, applications to interaction systems other than the coalition game will be considered. Before beginning this discussion, it should be made clear that although the decision situation can be reduced to a binary choice problem from the perspective of any individual member of the interaction systems that will be considered, the theory is not limited to binary choice decision situations. The theory can be applied to decision situations in which an individual selects from a set of N possible alternatives. For example, Siegel (Siegel et al., 1964, pp. 117–41) conducted an experiment in which subjects were required to predict the occurrence of three events that were defined by three different π parameters and for which two different payoffs were offered. The average absolute discrepancy between the model's predictions for choice strategies and observed strategies under these conditions was .011. The restriction of the application of the theory to problems that can be reduced to binary decisions is made so that the measurements of utility ratios obtained in the coalition researches can be employed. With different basic measurements (i.e., on three-alternative decisions, four-alternative decisions, etc.), more complex interaction problems could be just as readily explained.

Two applications of the theory will be considered. While these applications do not, by any means, exhaust the possibilities for types of situations to which the theory could be applied, they identify two important classes of social situations that can be conceptualized in terms of the general decision theory. The applications are to two-person conflicts and to N-person interaction systems.

11.1 APPLICATIONS TO TWO-PERSON CONFLICTS

The decision theory can be applied to any of the two-person, repetitive choice, zero or nonzero sum games considered in the literature of game theory. Since the application of the model is essentially the same for the entire class of game situations, the following discussion will take place in the context of the most well-known of the game situations, the prisoner's dilemma. The prisoner's dilemma decision problem is structured along the lines of the following description:

> Two suspects are taken into custody and separated. The district attorney is certain that they are guilty of a specific crime, but he does not have adequate evidence to convict them at a trial. He points out to each prisoner that each has two alternatives: to confess to the crime the police are sure they have done, or not to confess. If they both do not confess, then the district attorney states that he will book them on some very minor trumped-up charge, such as petty larceny and illegal possession of a weapon, and they both will receive minor punishment; if they both confess, they will be prosecuted, but he will recommend less than the most severe sentence; but if one confesses and the other does not, then the confessor will receive lenient treatment for turning state's evidence, whereas the latter will get "the book" slapped at him. (Luce and Raiffa, 1957, p. 95)

Each of the prisoners is faced with a binary decision, to confess or to remain silent. The outcome of selection of either course of action is dependent upon the behavior of the other prisoner. The game is therefore one which transpires between two individuals and in a situation in which a player's behavior will be very much influenced by his expectations about how his opponent will choose. The decision situation is further complicated by the fact that the best outcome for the pair, which comes about when each chooses not to confess, is less rewarding to a given prisoner than is the payoff that he obtains when he confesses and his opponent does not. A payoff matrix for the game described above could be the one in Figure 11.1.

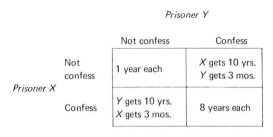

Prisoner Y

		Not confess	Confess
	Not confess	1 year each	X gets 10 yrs. Y gets 3 mos.
Prisoner X	Confess	Y gets 10 yrs. X gets 3 mos.	8 years each

Figure 11.1

In research on interpersonal conflict, the structural characteristics of the situation are preserved, although the prisoners are typically replaced with college students and the prison sentences are replaced with monetary payoffs. The dilemma faced by subjects in experimental investigations of conflict is analogous to the problem faced by the prisoners, since the relative payoffs are arranged such that a cooperative choice (no confession) yields a smaller payoff to each player than does a competitive choice (confession) when the other player chooses cooperation. Subjects are therefore tempted to defect from alliances in which both players choose the cooperative alternative. A typical payoff matrix is shown in Figure 11.2.

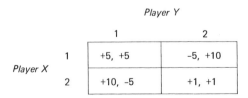

Player Y

		1	2
	1	+5, +5	-5, +10
Player X	2	+10, -5	+1, +1

Figure 11.2

The matrix is constructed such that the first entry in each cell is the payoff for player X. If players X and Y both choose alternative one, they each receive five dollars. If player X chooses one and Y chooses two, X loses five dollars and Y is paid 10 dollars.

Scodel et al. (1959) have defined the properties of the payoff matrix for a prisoner's dilemma game. For players one and two the payoffs for cooperative (alternative one) choices and competitive (alternative two) choices must satisfy the rules shown in Figure 11.3, where the first entry in each cell is the payoff for player one:

I. $2x_1 > x_2 + x_3 > 2x_4$
II. $x_3 > x_1$
III. $x_3 > x_2$
IV. $x_4 > x_2$

Player 2

		1	2
Player 1	1	$X_1 X_1$	$X_2 X_3$
	2	$X_3 X_2$	$X_4 X_4$

Figure 11.3

The game situation has become a focus of research for two reasons. The first is related to the issue of "rationality" in choice behavior, and the second is accounted for by the fact that the experimental situation is a convenient one in which to develop and test theories of cooperative and competitive behavior.

That portion of interest in the game situation that is related to the question of "rationality" centers around consideration of the fact that a player's safest strategy is to choose alternative two under all circumstances, while the best strategy to maximize gain for both participants in the game is to always choose alternative one. Except for the unlikely circumstance that an individual's opponent will permit him to make the alternative two choice while he continually chooses alternative one, the jointly cooperative strategy will maximize each individual's gains.

Luce and Raiffa have argued that for games with only a single play, there is nothing "irrational or perverse about the choice α_2 and β_2 [each player's alternative two], and we must admit that if we were actually in this position we would make these choices" (Luce and Raiffa, 1957, p. 96). When the game is iterated the analysis of the situation is substantially altered. Under this condition, it is proposed that "an unarticulated collusion between players will develop" (p. 101). The difference between expected behavior in single-play games and games with multiple iterations is accounted for by the fact that, with repeated plays, it is possible for two opponents to establish a pattern of behavior that results in greater benefit for each than would be achieved if both chose the uncooperative alternative.

It is the case, however, that even given the possibility of establishing a form of communication by signaling intent through consistent action, players do not "lock into" the cooperative, jointly and usually individually maximizing strategy. The problem that confronts researchers is to account for the display of a choice strategy that does not maximize the monetary payoffs available to players in the game.

The analysis of decision making in the prisoner's dilemma conflict situation that will be advanced here follows from application of the same theory that explained choice behavior in the light-guessing experiment and the coalition game. Although the prisoner's dilemma poses individuals with a type of problem quite different from those considered previously, we would argue that the classification of a concrete situation as one of interpersonal conflict or cooperation is irrelevant since the theory assumes that individuals will act so as to maximize expected utility in their decision making under all sets of circumstances.

It should be noted that the characteristics of a social setting that typically lead to its being classified as one of conflict or cooperation are properties of the manner in which payoffs are distributed for various outcomes. In the absence of a well-developed explanatory theory, the labels conflict and cooperation are convenient terms because they serve to imply certain expectations for how the payoff structure will affect interaction between players and how behavior is likely to be patterned. However, given a general theory of decision making that postulates maximization of expected utility, or any other general decision rule, the classification of a setting as one of conflict or cooperation does not assist in explaining behavior in the situation. In order to apply a theory based on assumptions of maximization of expected utility, it is sufficient to specify whether some factor increases the utility of a cooperative or a noncooperative response.

The analysis of the prisoner's dilemma game is based on identification of two sources of utility, the expected utility of an individual's alternative choices and the individual's utility for relative gain. (The expected utility of a choice is itself dependent on the payoff for making that choice and the probability of obtaining the payoffs.) It will be argued that the literature on the prisoner's dilemma conflict situation can be organized in terms of these factors and that the decision theory can be meaningfully applied.

I. EFFECTS OF PAYOFFS FOR COOPERATIVE AND NONCOOPERATIVE CHOICES

A player in a prisoner's dilemma game is faced with a series of binary decisions. He may only choose between the cooperative and noncoop-

erative alternatives. The choices of a given player are not, however, the sole
determinants of his payoffs and therefore of the expected utility of a choice.
The payoff a player obtains for each repetition of the game is a function of the
joint action of both participants. For purposes of analysis, it is necessary to
treat the effects of the payoffs independently of the probabilistic aspects of the
game situation. Consider the matrix in Figure 11.4.

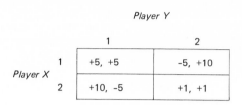

Player Y

	1	2
1	+5, +5	-5, +10
2	+10, -5	+1, +1

Player X (label to the left, row 1 and row 2)

Figure 11.4

If player X chooses alternative one his payoff will be either plus or
minus five $[X_1 = (+5, -5)]$, and if he chooses alternative two it will be
either plus 10 or plus one $[X_2 = (+10, +1)]$. The payoffs for alternatives
are unequal, and in one case the possible wins and losses are balanced
(alternative one), while in the other case they are unbalanced (alternative
two).

The manner in which payoffs are associated with alternatives is quite
similar to the format used by Siegel in his research in the context of the
light-guessing situation. In Siegel's experiment with unequal alpha payoff
conditions, the procedure was to pay a subject a certain amount if he correctly
predicted the occurrence of an event and to deduct an equivalent amount if
his prediction was incorrect. In the context of the light-guessing experiment
the payoffs might have been defined such that if the subject predicted event
one and was correct, his payoff was plus five. If he predicted event one and
was incorrect, his payoff was minus five. This is identical to the payoff
structure for a cooperative choice under the conditions of the prisoner's
dilemma game illustrated above. If player X chooses alternative one and so
does his opponent, he wins five points. If player X chooses alternative one and
his opponent chooses the noncooperative alternative (number two), X loses
five points. In the light-guessing experiments it was always the case that the
amounts of possible wins and losses for a given choice were equal but of
opposite signs. Although varying this condition complicates the subject's
decision problem, the formal structure of the model permits such a variation.
It should be clear that in terms of an individual's payoffs for various outcomes
of decisions, the prisoner's dilemma game is not radically different from the
structure of the decision problems already treated in previous applications
of the theory.

The effects of differences in the expected utility of a choice can most clearly be observed through comparison of the choice strategies adopted by subjects who play the game with matrices that differ only with regard to the payoffs for one of the alternative decisions, but play against robots that operate with identical probabilities of alternative choices. Compare the payoff matrix in Figure 11.5 with the one in Figure 11.4. In this case, for

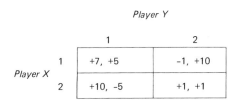

Player Y

		1	2
	1	+7, +5	-1, +10
Player X			
	2	+10, -5	+1, +1

Figure 11.5

player X the cooperative choice yields either a plus seven or a minus one payoff [$X_1 = (+7, -1)$], and the noncooperative alternative pays either plus 10 or plus one [$X_2 = (+10, +1)$]. The differences between the first matrix (Figure 11.4) and the one in Figure 11.5 affect only the payoffs for a cooperative choice. Under the conditions of the second matrix, player X receives a greater positive payoff when he and Y choose to cooperate, and he loses less when he chooses to cooperate and Y makes a noncooperative choice. The specific differences between payoffs are that under the conditions of the first matrix $X_1 = (+5, -5)$, while under the conditions of the second matrix $X_1 = (+7, -1)$. Therefore, with the second matrix, a jointly cooperative choice yields a two-point greater payoff for player X, and for making a cooperative choice that is not reciprocated by player Y, player X is penalized four points less.

In comparison with the first matrix, the second matrix has a greater expected utility for a cooperative choice. Given any distribution of choices by player Y, player X's expected payoff for an alternative one choice is greater under the conditions of the second matrix than it was under the payoffs specified by the first matrix. Since it is assumed that expected utility is directly related to expected payoff, the expected utility of an alternative one choice would be greater under the conditions of the second matrix. The theoretical expectation would therefore be a greater probability of selection of the cooperative alternative under the conditions of the second matrix.

A number of studies have been conducted in which payoffs have been systematically varied while the behavior of the subject's robot opponent was held constant. Bixenstine and Blundell (1966) conducted several experiments in which subjects played against identical robot strategies. In some of their treatment conditions only the payoffs associated with one of the subject's alternative choices were varied. In one condition, payoffs were assigned as follows:

$$X_1 = (+3, -3)$$
$$X_2 = (+6, 0)$$

In a second condition, only the payoffs for a cooperative choice were altered. Subjects played against an identical robot strategy in both treatment conditions. Payoffs in the second condition were:

$$X_1 = (+3, -3)$$
$$X_2 = (-3, 0)$$

The relevant theoretical difference between conditions was a decrease in the expected utility of a choice of alternative two. The difference between the choice strategies of individuals who played against the same simulated opponent under the conditions of the two matrices was a smaller probability of an alternative two choice under the conditions of the second matrix.

Numerous studies have been conducted in which payoffs have been systematically altered and in which there were two subjects, rather than one subject and a preprogrammed robot (Minas et al., 1960; Scodel et al., 1959; Lave, 1965; Radlow, 1965; and Gallo and McClintock, 1965). Although the opponent's strategy cannot be strictly controlled under these circumstances, the effects of changes in payoffs can be specified.

The most extensive research program treating the conflict situation is reported by Rapoport and Chammah (1965). The results of experiments with seven different matrices are reported. When comparisons are made between the observed decision strategies of subjects playing under payoff conditions that differ in the manner illustrated above, the result is that the distribution of choices between the cooperative and noncooperative alternatives varies as a function of the expected utilities of the alternatives. For example, in a set of treatment conditions subjects were confronted with payoffs that varied in only one respect. The payoff for a jointly cooperative outcome was systematically increased while the payoffs for all other outcomes were held constant. The three sets of payoffs are reported in Table 11.1. The payoffs in the three conditions differ only with regard to the utility of a cooperative outcome. In Condition I, the subject received either plus one or minus 10 for a cooperative choice. In Condition II, the possible payoffs were plus five or minus 10. In the third condition, the payoffs were either plus nine or minus 10. Theoretically, the increase in payoff for a jointly cooperative outcome should have resulted in an increase in the expected utility of an alternative one choice across conditions. This increase in expected utility should, according to the theory, have resulted in a corresponding increase in the probability of an alternative one choice by subjects. The mean probabilities of alternative one choices reported in Table 11.1 indicate that this is precisely the result. Across Conditions I through III the probabilities of cooperative choices change from .458 to .635 to .734.

Table 11.1 *Effects of Variation of Payoffs for Alternative Choices*

Condition	Payoffs for choices 1 and 2	Probabilities of alternative choices
I	1 = (+1, −10)	P_1 = .458
	2 = (+10, −1)	P_2 = .542
II	1 = (+5, −10)	P_1 = .635
	2 = (+10, −1)	P_2 = .365
III	1 = (+9, −10)	P_1 = .734
	2 = (+10, −1)	P_2 = .266

II. EFFECTS OF PROBABILISTIC CONSIDERATIONS

The expected utility of choice is a product of two variables, the utility of the payoffs associated with the chosen alternative and the probability of obtaining the payoffs. In the preceding section the utilities of payoffs were considered independently of probabilistic considerations. The reverse case will be considered in this section.

The probability with which a payoff is obtained depends on the behavior of the individual's opponent. When robots are used to simulate the subject's opponent their behaviors are typically determined in one of two fashions. In some studies (Minas et al., 1960; Bixenstine et al., 1963; Lave, 1965; Shure and Meeker, 1968) the behavior of the robot is determined by a choice parameter (e.g., selection of alternative one with probability .80 and alternative two with probability .20). In other studies (Loomis, 1959; Scodel, 1962; Bixenstine et al., 1963; Lave, 1965) the behavior of the robot was contingent on the behavior of the subject or the point in the experiment. For example, in a study by Bixenstine and his associates (1963) subjects played against an opponent who matched the subject's choice on 83% of the trials and mismatched on the remaining 17%. In a study by Loomis (1959) subjects played against a simulated opponent who played cooperatively on the first trial and thereafter matched the subject's choice. Finally, in an experiment by

Lave (1965) the robot was programmed so that it moved from the noncooperative alternative to the cooperative choice only after a series of five sequential cooperative choices by the subject.

It is difficult to evaluate the results of experiments run with the second method of robot control since they are actually concerned with responses to patterns of play. The first procedure for robot management yields data that are of greater value for the current enterprise. Even evaluation of this data is somewhat difficult, however, since researchers have tended to use extreme parameter values for the robots' choice behavior. The danger in this practice is that since the robot's behavior on trial $N + 1$ is not contingent on the subject's choice on trial N, and since the robot adopts an extreme position, the subject may discover that he faces a rather strange opponent.

Consider a subject faced with a robot opponent that chooses the cooperative alternative on 95% of the trials. This means that the robot will choose the noncooperative alternative only once in 20 iterations of the game. Assume that at the start both players choose the cooperative alternative. At some point, say trial 10, the robot must make a noncooperative response. It is likely that the subject will react to the defection by following suit on trial 11. On this same trial, number 11, the robot will make a cooperative choice. Having chosen to retaliate against his opponent on trial 11 and finding that the robot has returned to the cooperative choice, the subject might reasonably decide to repeat his noncooperative choice on trial 12 in order to guard against retaliation by his opponent or to inflict further punishment for the initial defection. If the subject does this he is in a position to discover that his opponent is somewhat strange. The subject will find that he can continue to exploit his opponent and is only retaliated against on one out of 20 trials. The effects of an extreme strategy can be seen even more clearly under circumstances in which the subject makes the first defection from the cooperative alliance. If at trial three the subject chooses alternative two, he will find that the robot does not retaliate until trial 10 and then makes only a single aggressive response before returning to the cooperative alternative.

Contrast this situation to one in which a human opponent adopts a highly cooperative choice strategy but occasionally defects and always retaliates against defection in a sensible fashion. This is a vastly different psychological situation from one that confronts an individual who plays against a robot which, except for rare defections, is unconditionally cooperative and takes no notice of being exploited.

The effect of an extreme strategy can be clearly seen in some data reported by Shure and Meeker (1968).[1] The same payoff matrix was used in treatment conditions for two sets of subjects who were randomly assigned to experimental conditions. In one condition there were two human subjects.

1. The authors wish to thank Gerald Shure and Robert Meeker for making this data available.

In the other condition the subject played against a robot that chose the cooperative alternative with a probability of .80. The results of the experiment were reported in graphic form with data points calculated for 10-trial blocks. The curves for the two groups of subjects are reported in Figure 11.6.

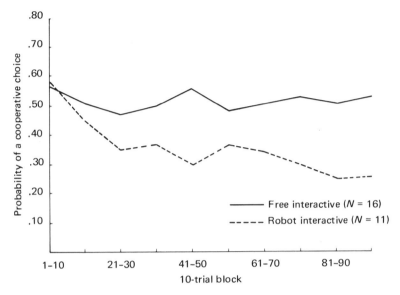

Figure 11.6 *Effects of Extreme Robot Parameter Values.*

Observe the difference between conditions. For the first 10 trials subjects in both conditions exhibit nearly identical probabilities of cooperative choices. For the remainder of the experiment, however, the differences between the free-play (two human subjects) and robot conditions are quite pronounced. Until stabilization in the last 20 trials of the experiment there is an increasing tendency for subjects in the robot interactive condition to exploit their opponents. Subjects in the free-play condition maintain approximately the same choice strategy throughout the experiment.

Additional indications of distortion of results due to selection of extreme parameter values for robots are given by the following set of results. Under conditions of free play with symmetric payoff matrices there is an extremely strong tendency for subjects to adopt matching choice strategies (identical probabilities of alternative choices). This can be clearly seen in data reported by Rapoport and Chammah (1965). They present the results of two experiments in which pairs of males and pairs of females play the prisoner's dilemma game under identical matrix conditions. Although, as noted previously, there were mean differences between populations with regard to the probability levels at which they stabilized their choice strategies, the data reported on probabilities through time reveal that players within each condition tended to almost perfectly match their opponents' choice strategies.

If in robot-interactive games the behavior of the robot is set at less than an extreme value, the tendency for subjects to match is only slightly disturbed. In a study discussed in Chapter 4, data obtained by Lieberman (1962) were reported. In a matrix game experiment the robot choice strategy was set at .75—.25. The graphs reported previously (p. 25) reveal that subjects tend to match the robot's behavior with a degree of accuracy somewhat less than that displayed by subjects in the Rapoport and Chammah experiments. When the robot's choice strategy is set at an extreme value and is not contingent on the subject's response, the distortion is considerable. For example, a study by Bixenstine et al. (1963) reports the results of setting the robot's strategy at an unconditionally cooperative response (probability equal to one). Under these conditions, subjects choose the cooperative alternative with a probability of only .39.

Although the issues raised above make evaluation of the existing research on probabilistic effects somewhat difficult, they do not completely preclude analysis of the effects of systematic differences in robot choice strategies. Studies by Minas et al. (1960), Scodel (1962), Bixenstine et al. (1963), and Shure and Meeker (1968) have investigated the effects of different robot strategies on the probabilities of choices by subjects. In two of these studies, Minas et al. (1960) and Bixenstine et al. (1963), the same payoff matrix was used and a total of three different sets of robot parameter values were employed. Although for the requirements of the analysis presently being conducted there were certain serious problems with these studies (the problems will be discussed shortly), they provide an opportunity to evaluate the effects of three different robot choice strategies on subject choice strategies in the prisoner's dilemma game.

The robot parameters, payoffs for alternative choices, and subject choice strategies are summarized in Table 11.2. The probability of a cooperative choice by the robot was reduced across the three conditions from unconditional cooperation (probability equal to one) to .87 to .17. Since the expected utility of an alternative varies directly with the probability of its occurrence, the theory would predict that the probability of the subject making a cooperative choice would vary directly with the robot's probability value. The reactions of subjects to the three robot strategies were probabilities of cooperative choices of .39, .33, and .30. The differences between subject strategies are in the predicted order although not large in an absolute sense.

Other experimenters have obtained more substantial differences in subject strategies with smaller changes in robot parameters. Shure and Meeker (1968), for example, conducted an experiment in which, in one

Table 11.2 *Effects of Variation in the Robot's Choice Strategy*

Condition	Probabilities of alternative choices by robots	Probabilities of alternative choices by subjects
I	1 = 1	.39
	2 = 0	.61
II	1 = .83	.33
	2 = .17	.67
III	1 = .17	.30
	2 = .83	.70

condition, the robot chose the cooperative alternative with a probability of .80, and in the second condition the robot chose this alternative with a probability of .20. The mean probability of a cooperative choice by subjects in the first condition was .36 and in the second condition it was .22. The most impressive aspect of the result is that the difference between conditions was highly consistent through the course of the experiment. The experiment was iterated 100 times, and with blocks of as few as 10 trials the difference between conditions is clearly consistent (see Table 11.3).

The effects of the parameters of the robot's choice strategy can be further analyzed by considering reactions to changes in parameter values during the course of a single experiment. In a study by Bixenstine and Wilson (1963) the probability of a cooperative choice was varied over a range from .95 to .05 during the experiment. The results demonstrate that subjects vary their strategies with those of the robot. The clearest data on this point is provided by Lieberman (1962); the relevant data (see Chapter 4, p. 24) demonstrates the high degree of sensitivity to changes in the robot's outputs.

III. EFFECTS OF THE DESIRE FOR RELATIVE GAIN

The distinction between single-play and iterated games is crucial in understanding the effects of the variable of utility for relative gain in the explanation of decision making in the prisoner's dilemma game. The classic analysis of the game situation that results in specification of a noncooperative choice as the "rational" decision is quite correct for single-play games. The problem there is to minimize possible losses, and the only safe strategy is to make the noncooperative choice. It has been shown empirically that when experimental conditions approximate the theoretical conditions for which this conclusion is appropriate, the result is quite close to game theoretic

Table 11.3 *Effects of Different Robot Parameters Through Time*

Condition	N	Robot parameter		Probability of alternative one choice by subjects in 10-trial blocks									
		P_1	P_2	1	2	3	4	5	6	7	8	9	10
I	11	.80	.20	.58	.45	.35	.37	.30	.37	.34	.30	.25	.24
II	9	.20	.80	.41	.27	.24	.27	.19	.22	.24	.16	.14	.10
I − II =				.17	.18	.11	.10	.11	.15	.10	.14	.11	.14

expectations. In a recent study (Shure and Meeker, 1968) prisoner's dilemma games were conducted in which subjects participated in groups of up to 24 individuals. Each subject was seated at a computer-operated teletype and was told that he would play the game for a large number of trials. Subjects were also informed that they would change opponents after every iteration of the game. This discontinuity in interaction served to effectively prevent the possibility of establishing any form of communication between players and therefore approximated the conditions of single-play games. Shure and Meeker report that by the last 10-trial block of the experiment, fully 88% of the subjects were choosing the noncooperative alternative with probability one.

The analysis of repeated-play prisoner's dilemma games leads to the conclusion that, at least for games in which the number of trials is not known, the "rational" strategy is for both players to cooperate completely and for each to choose the first alternative with probability one. Using the payoffs specified in the illustrative matrix discussed at the beginning of the analysis of two person conflicts (Figure 11.2),

$$X_1 = (+5, -5)$$
$$X_2 = (+10, +1)$$

if both players choose the cooperative alternative with probability one, each player's expected payoff is $+500$ over a series of 100 iterations of the game, $[(1)(+5)(100)]$. If both players adopt choice strategies that are equally cooperative but with only a .75 probability of a cooperative choice, each player's expected payoff would be $+381$, $[\{(.75)(.75)(+5) + (.75)(.25)(-5) + (.25)(.75)(+10) + (.25)(.25)(+1)\}(100)]$.

There is more than sufficient data available to demonstrate that subjects do not adopt the monetarily maximizing strategy of selection of the cooperative alternative with probability one. For example, in the extensive research program conducted by Rapoport and Chammah (1965), seven different matrices were used in games with two human players. The matrices varied greatly in payoffs associated with different outcomes. The mean probability of a cooperative response for the 140 subjects over all matrices and for the 300 iterations of the game was .59.

The theoretical problem is to account for the deviation from the strict monetarily maximizing strategy of a probability one cooperative choice. Results of research in both the prisoner's dilemma game situation and in various other social-psychological studies suggest that subjects depart from the purely cooperative strategy in order to produce an outcome to the experiment such that they accumulate a higher score than do their opponents. That is, subjects behave as if there exists a utility for relative gain, and they are willing to win less money (points, etc.) if they are able to differentiate their performance from that of their opponent's and produce a relatively better score. In keeping with the terminology of the formal model, the desire for relative gain results in a utility for choice variability. The utility for choice variability stemming from relative gain may be formally treated in the same manner as was the utility for choice variability arising from boredom in the light-guessing experiment and from desires for equity in the coalition game.

The magnitude of utility for relative gain with which a subject operates in a given experiment is likely to vary as a function of several variables. For example, as Festinger (1954) has argued, individuals desire to evaluate both their opinions and abilities. This suggests that the more the pre-game instructions define the game as a competitive situation, the more subjects will attempt to demonstrate their competitive abilities.

In two studies by Deutsch (1958, 1960), the subject's definition of the situation was manipulated. In the first experiment, three motivational states were induced. Pre-game instructions to subjects stressed either (1) that the proper concern of players was the welfare of both participants, (2) that each player should be concerned only with his own outcomes, or (3) that each player should be concerned with both doing well for himself and better than his opponent. The results of the experiment reveal that choice strategies varied with treatment condition in the expected manner. The second study (Deutsch, 1960) reports results consistent with the earlier research.

Several studies have shown that certain attitude or personality characteristics of subjects are related to the degree to which they attempt to differentiate their performances from those of their opponents (cf. Lutzker, 1960; McClintock et al., 1963; Bixenstine et al., 1963; Bixenstine and Wilson, 1963). Lutzker (1960), for example, demonstrated that subjects who differed with regard to attitudes toward political isolationism adopted different choice strategies in the game situation.

It has been postulated that the utility for relative gain is related to the choice strategy adopted by a subject and that a subject's utility for relative gain can be manipulated by changing characteristics of the game situation. It would be reasonable to expect that utility for relative gain would be inversely related to group cohesiveness. A number of studies (Deutsch, 1958; Wilson et al., 1964; Gallo and McClintook, 1965; Oskamp and Perlman, 1965; Radlow, 1965) have reported the effects of different levels of cohesiveness on the probability of a noncooperative response.

Oskamp and Perlman (1965) report that subjects who were made to interact with confederates prior to playing the game exhibited a more cooperative choice strategy than those who had had no prior interaction. In an interesting experiment by Wilson et al. (1964) the experimenter manipulated cohesiveness by having teams of subjects jointly make decisions in a game against another team and also had team members play against each other in order to determine the division of team winnings. The creation of in-group solidarity resulted in a high probability of a cooperative choice in the game against the teammate. The play of the game against the other team was highly competitive.

The theoretical explanation for this result would be that making two individuals members of a team leads to their assigning a relatively small utility to relative gain over their teammates. Creating an opposing team leads to a relatively great utility for demonstrating superiority over the opposing team. In the experiments the probability of a competitive choice against the opposing team was approximately twice that of a competitive choice in games against teammates.

Given the analysis of the existing prisoner's dilemma game literature in terms of probabilistic considerations and two sources of utility, the choice model can be applied to the game situation. Participants in a prisoner's dilemma game are confronted with a choice situation in which they are conceived of as attempting to maximize the combination of utilities stemming from payoffs associated with outcomes of choices and utilities stemming from desires to demonstrate superiority over their opponents. The formal model for decision making in the game is as follows.

Let π_i = the probability that the opponent chooses alternative i, $i = 1, 2$,

a_i = the marginal utility of the payoff for choice i, $i = 1, 2$,

b = the marginal utility of relative gain,

α_i = the ratio a_i/b_i, $i = 1, 2$, and

P_i = the stable-state probability that the player chooses alternative i, $i = 1, 2$.

Following the derivation presented in Chapter 3, the final equations of the model are:

$$P_1 = \tfrac{1}{4}(\alpha_1\pi_1 - \alpha_2\pi_2) + \tfrac{1}{2}$$
$$P_2 = 1 - P_1$$

The choice theory has not been empirically tested in a research program specifically designed for the evaluation of its power in the context of the prisoner's dilemma game. However, there does exist in the literature a set of three experiments in which the same payoff matrix was used, the behavior of one of the players was simulated, and the π parameters were varied in a manner which permits application of the model.

Application of the model to this data is not strictly appropriate since certain necessary experimental conditions for its application were not achieved in the researches. For example, the published data report only the mean probabilities of alternative one and two choices for 30 trials in two experiments and for 50 trials in the third experiment. It is impossible, from this data, to judge the point at which a stable-state choice strategy is attained if it is attained during the experiment. Therefore, in order to use this data at all, the model must be applied to the data from the entire length of the experiment.

A second consideration is that the data were gathered by two different teams of researchers, and the procedures under which the experiments were run differed between experiments. In light of the assumption that the magnitude of utility assigned to relative gain varies with the set of instructions employed by the researcher, this is a serious problem.

The third point is that in all three treatment conditions extreme robot choice parameters were selected. As noted earlier, extreme robot behaviors are likely to produce somewhat distorted reactions by subjects and therefore are likely to make the utility estimates less reliable than is usually the case.

The final point is that the researches were carried out at two different universities, and therefore subjects for the three treatment conditions were not drawn from the same population. Since application of the model rests on the empirical condition that subjects in different treatment conditions assign the same average utility to the payoffs and to relative gain, combining data from different populations without random assignment to treatment conditions might be quite dangerous.

Students at different institutions could differ substantially in their assignments of utility to the monetary payoffs and to relative gain. For example, Lave (1965) conducted three separate but identical prisoner's dilemma experiments with students at Harvard, M.I.T., and Northeastern University. The choice strategies adopted by Harvard and M.I.T. students were identical, while the strategies displayed by Northeastern students were substantially different. In the applications of the model to the light-guessing experiment and the coalition game, subjects were sampled from a single population and randomly assigned to treatment conditions in order to control for individual variation in assignment of utilities. In the published researches on the prisoner's dilemma game this procedure was not employed.[2]

Although there are many reasons why the data from these experiments are less than an ideal set with which to test the theory, they are the only set found in the literature that provides even the remotest possibility of use. Application of the model to these data provides only the most preliminary test of the model's ability to predict decision making in the prisoner's dilemma situation.

The data to which the model will be applied were reported by Minas et al. (1960) and Bixenstine et al. (1963). Table 11.4 summarizes the characteristics of the three treatment conditions. Observe that the payoffs for

---

2. The two teams of researchers were, of course, conducting the experiments for their own purposes, and there was no reason to employ procedures that would permit an unambiguous test of the model being considered here.

alternative choices are held constant across conditions and that the π parameters for the robot with which subjects interacted were varied from unconditional cooperation to a .17 probability of a cooperative choice.

Table 11.4 *Formal Characteristics of Decision-Making Experiments in the Prisoner's Dilemma Game*

Condition	Probabilities of robot selections of alternatives 1 and 2		Payoffs for alternatives 1 and 2		Number of subjects	Number of trials
	π_1	π_2	a_1	a_2		
I	1.0	0	(3, 0)	(5, 1)	26	50
II	.83	.17	(3, 0)	(5, 1)	12	30
III	.17	.83	(3, 0)	(5, 1)	12	30

Since this application of the theory is intended to provide only preliminary results (such as does the model accurately predict the direction of differences between conditions, etc.), and there are severe problems with the design of the experiments, it was decided to use all of the available data in order to estimate utility ratios. The procedure for accomplishing the requisite measurements is described in Chapter 9 and in Appendix I. The results of applying the model to the prisoner's dilemma data are presented in Table 11.5.

The model's predictions for the maximizing choice strategies are quite close to those displayed by subjects. For example, in Condition I the pre-

Table 11.5 *Application of the Decision Theory to Interaction in the Prisoner's Dilemma Game*

Condition	Predicted* P_1 and P_2	Observed P_1 and P_2	|Discrepancy|
I	$P_1 = .365$	.385	.020
	$P_2 = .635$	.615	
II	$P_1 = .351$	.333	.018
	$P_2 = .649$	.667	
III	$P_1 = .299$	.303	.004
	$P_2 = .701$	.697	

*The estimated alpha ratios for alternative choices were $\alpha_1 = -.54113$ and $\alpha_2 = .85663$.

dicted choice strategy is to choose the cooperative alternative with a probability of .365 and the noncooperative alternative with probability .635. The strategy adopted by subjects in the Condition I treatment was $P_1 = .385$ and $P_2 = .615$. The absolute discrepancy between the observed and predicted strategies was .020. This was the largest discrepancy between predicted and observed strategies for the three conditions. The absolute discrepancy in Condition II was .018 and in Condition III it was .004.

Since all of the available data were used in the alpha estimating procedure, the application of the theory to this data from the prisoner's dilemma game does not constitute a test of the model in the same sense as did the previous applications to the data from the coalition games. The present application demonstrates that this model can describe the data with reasonable accuracy. If this were not true, it would be out of the question to seriously consider the decision theory as providing a possible explanation of behavior under the conditions of the prisoner's dilemma game. The accuracy with which the model's predictions fit the data is strong support for continuing research on interpersonal conflict through application of the decision theory.

The choice model can be applied to freely interactive conflict situations as well as to games in which a subject interacts with a robot. Application of the model to freely interactive two-person conflicts is logically identical to the generalization to freely interactive coalition games. The generalization to the two-person conflict situation is as follows. Where P_{Ai} equals the probability that a player (A) chooses the ith alternative ($i = 1, 2$) and π_{Ai} equals the probability that a player (A) chose the ith alternative ($i = 1, 2$), the stable-state choice strategies for players X and Y in a freely interactive prisoner's dilemma game are given in the following equations.

$$P_{X1} = \tfrac{1}{4}(\alpha_1 \pi_{Y1} - \alpha_2 \pi_{Y2}) + .5$$
$$P_{Y1} = \tfrac{1}{4}(\alpha_1 \pi_{X1} - \alpha_2 \pi_{X2}) + .5$$

Replacing π terms with P terms, we obtain:

$$P_{X1} = \tfrac{1}{4}(\alpha_1 P_{Y1} - \alpha_2 + \alpha_2 P_{Y1}) + .5$$
$$P_{Y1} = \tfrac{1}{4}(\alpha_1 P_{X1} - \alpha_2 + \alpha_2 P_{X1}) + .5$$

Therefore:

$$4P_{X1} = (\alpha_1 + \alpha_2) P_{Y1} - \alpha_2 + 2$$
$$4P_{Y1} = (\alpha_1 + \alpha_2) P_{X1} - \alpha_2 + 2$$

Written as a system of simultaneous linear equations, these become:

$$4P_{X1} - (\alpha_1 + \alpha_2) P_{Y1} = 2 - \alpha_2$$
$$(\alpha_1 + \alpha_2)P_{X1} - 4P_{Y1} = -2 + \alpha_2$$

If the alpha estimates calculated from the data reported in Table 11.5 are introduced, a prediction can be arrived at for the stable-state choice strategies that would be adopted by subjects playing the game under the payoff conditions described in Table 11.4. Under these conditions the maximizing strategies for each player would be to distribute choices as follows.

$$P_1 = .310$$

$$P_2 = .690$$

Although there are no available data against which to test the model's predictions, there is one point on which the prediction is consistent with results reported for behavior in freely interactive prisoner's dilemma games. Note that the model predicts that players who operate with identical utility ratios will adopt identical choice strategies (in the example, each will select the cooperative alternative with a probability of .310 and the noncooperative alternative with probability .690). Data reported by Rapoport and Chammah (1965, pp. 185–97) reveal that there is a strong tendency for players in games against opponents of the same sex to adopt identical choice strategies, precisely as the model would predict.

11.2 APPLICATIONS TO *N*-PERSON SYSTEMS

It was noted earlier that the decision theory is not restricted to binary choice problems and is not limited to a maximum of three-person interaction systems. There is, however, an empirical limitation on the applications of the formal model that can be made at the present time since the prerequisite utility measurements have been carried out for only binary decisions and with only certain payoff and equity constants in operation. Rather than attempt to discuss the range of interaction systems to which the theory could be applied if additional measurements were obtained, the following discussion will be restricted to applications that can be carried out with the utility ratios that have already been measured. Hopefully, the further extensions that could be made with additional basic measurements will be obvious.

Two types of *N*-person systems will be considered. These are simple chains and complex networks. The differences between these systems are in terms of properties of the structure in which interaction occurs. In a formal sense the theory is indifferent to the manner in which individuals are interconnected (social structures), providing that the necessary restrictions on the decision problems confronting each participant are enforced (number of alternatives, equity manipulation, etc.). This is not to say, however, that structure is an unimportant consideration. While structural variations will have substantial effects on the resultant behavior of the system, they need not be considered in any explicit fashion in the application of the theory to an interaction system.

The applications of the theory to the decision making of individuals and to the behavior of complex interaction systems as a whole will be couched in terms of the formation of coalitions between members of the system. The discussions are restricted to this context solely because the bulk of the researches on which these applications rest were carried out in the context of coalition formation problems. The theory is in no way limited to this context, as the previous applications to the nonsocial decision problem and to two-person conflict situations have shown. In its most general sense the decision problem facing members of the systems to be discussed is one of coordinating their behaviors to the behaviors of other members of the system in a situation in which there is true interaction between system members and true conflict of interest between individuals. The theory will be employed in order to conceptualize and predict both the behavior of individuals interacting in the context of complex social structures and the behavior of systems of interacting individuals, and as a tool to be used in the analysis of properties of social structures.

With regard to the third item, the analysis of properties of social structures, the model can be employed to determine the relative structurally determined power of the occupant of a particular position to influence the behaviors of the other members of the system. The term "structurally determined power" is intended to denote that portion of an individual's ability to affect the behaviors of the other members of a system that derives from the position he occupies in that system. It has long been recognized that the manner in which a position in a social structure is related to the other positions affects the degree to which the occupant of that position can affect the behavior of the occupants of other positions within the structure. It will be shown below that the model provides a tool that may be used to discover the degree to which positions in a social structure possess structurally determined power.

I. INTERACTION CHAINS

Consider an interaction structure of the type represented in Figure 11.7.

The system represented in Figure 11.7 is a five-position interaction chain. The term chain is applied to this structure for two reasons. First, occupants of each position are in direct interaction with only a subset of the members of the system, and second, in terms of the structure's formal properties when represented as a graph, in order for any path to return to its point of origin in

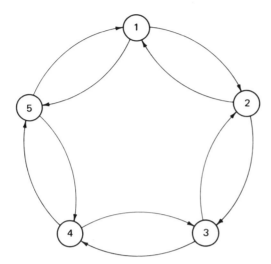

Figure 11.7 *A Five-Position Interaction Chain.* The notation for representation of *N*-person chains is different from that employed to represent three-person games. The directed lines connecting points represent communication channels between individuals. For example, positions one and two are connected by a directed line originating from each position. The relations between the occupants of the positions are that individual one's decisions are communicated to individual two, and two's decisions are communicated to player one. The choice problem confronting a member of the system is to coordinate his behaviors to those of the individuals with whom he communicates. For example, the occupant of position number one must attempt to form coalitions with the occupants of positions two and five.

more than two steps and without passing through the same point twice, it is necessary that it pass through all the points of the graph.

In the structure represented in Figure 11.7 each member of the system is in interaction with two other participants. Assume that, as in the coalition game, the rules governing interactions between participants require each individual to make a binary decision on each of a series of trials.[3] If on a given

3. In order to employ the utility constants that have already been estimated, it would be necessary for the experimental situation to be defined to players in the same manner as were the three-person coalition games. In fact, the best manner in which to ensure that the utility constants were applicable would be to inform subjects that they were going to play a three-person coalition game, use the same instructions and payoffs that were employed in the previous researches, and then interconnect players in the manner diagrammed in Figure 11.7. If the alternative procedure were used (informing subjects of the true structure of the game), it would require conducting new measurement experiments in order to estimate the appropriate utility ratios to be safe. Since the change from a three-person

trial player one selects player two and two selects player one, they would have formed a coalition for that trial and each would receive some predetermined payoff.

The chain structure is a straightforward extension of the structure of a three-person coalition game and differs in only one major respect. The three-person coalition game is a special case. It is one of the two interaction systems in which participants make only binary decisions and in which each player may be in direct communication with every other player.[4] In chain type structures position occupants are related to at least some of the system members in only an indirect fashion. For example, the occupant of position number one (in Figure 11.7) has no direct interaction with the occupant of position number three. He is, however, in interaction with player two who is in turn in interaction with player three. Changes in player one's behavior will affect player two's decision strategy and this will in turn affect player three's behavior. Players one and three can be considered to be indirectly related to one another in the sense that a change in either individual's behavior can affect the behavior of the other.

In order to apply the model to the interaction structure represented in Figure 11.7, all that is necessary is to define the payoffs that each participant receives if he is able to successfully coordinate his decision strategy to the behaviors of the individuals with whom he is in interaction. Figure 11.8 presents a reproduction of the interaction structure with the addition of a set of payoffs for each of the participants. The convention for reading the notation indicating payoffs is that a player receives the payoff associated with an input channel if he correctly predicts when the player who uses that channel selects him. For example, player one receives 10 cents if he correctly predicts that player two will select him on some trial. Player two receives five cents if he correctly predicts that player one will select him on some iteration of the game. In the structure represented in Figure 11.8 the occupant of position number one is the only player who has a preference between alternative coalitions. The other members of the system are offered equal payoffs for alternative coalitions and therefore are economically indifferent to alternatives.

---

coalition game to a chain does not entail changes that would obviously affect utility assignments, providing that the payoffs and the equity inducing aspects of the instructions are held constant, it might be that subjects could be informed of the true structure of the interaction system and of the previously measured constants still employed. This could be empirically tested with a simple experiment. Lacking such a demonstration, however, the discussions of applications of the model to N-person systems will be based on the assumption that subjects are instructed in the same manner as were participants in the coalition game researches.

4. The only other interaction structure in which all participants are in direct interaction and individuals make only binary decisions is a two-person interaction.

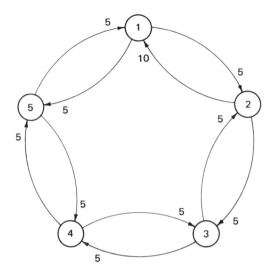

Figure 11.8 *A Chain Structure with Payoffs to Players.*

The generalized form of the decision theory can be applied to the structure represented in Figure 11.3 and the behavior of the interaction system described by the following system of simultaneous linear equations:

$$4P_{1,2} - \alpha_{1,2}P_{2,1} \qquad\qquad + \alpha_{1,5}P_{5,1} = 2$$
$$\alpha_{2,1}P_{1,2} - 4P_{2,1} - \alpha_{2,3}P_{3,2} \qquad\qquad = -2$$
$$-\alpha_{3,2}P_{2,1} - 4P_{3,2} - \alpha_{3,4}P_{4,3} \qquad = -2 - \alpha_{3,2}$$
$$-\alpha_{4,3}P_{3,2} - 4P_{4,3} + \alpha_{4,5}P_{5,1} = -2 - \alpha_{4,3} + \alpha_{4,5}$$
$$\alpha_{5,1}P_{1,2} \qquad - \alpha_{5,4}P_{4,3} + 4P_{5,1} = 2 + \alpha_{5,1} - \alpha_{5,4}$$

Given estimates of utility ratios for the payoffs to system members for correct predictions of the behaviors of the individuals with whom they are in interaction, the model yields a prediction for the equilibrium point to which the interaction system will move. Solutions for the utility-maximizing strategy for each member of the system result in prediction of the equilibrium point described in Figure 11.9.

The predicted equilibrium point for the system is in no sense obvious. The most interesting aspect of the model's prediction is for the behavior that will be adopted by the occupant of position one. Player one is the only member of the system who is offered unequal payoffs. He receives 10 cents for forming a coalition with player number two and five cents for a coalition with player number five. Intuitively, it would be expected that player one would be oriented toward forming coalitions with player two. The structure of the interaction system is such, however, that his maximizing choice strategy is to choose player two with a probability of only .24 and player five with a probability of .76. In terms of the properties of the interaction structure, the

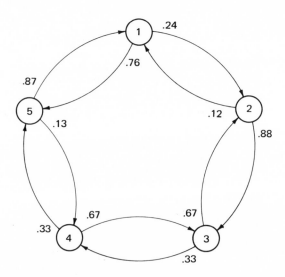

Figure 11.9 *An Equilibrium Point for a Five-Position Chain.* The convention for reading the figure is that the probability with which an individual (*X*) chooses another player (*Y*) is the value associated with the directed line leading from *X*'s position to *Y*'s.

equilibrium predictions for the system suggest that the structure controls the behaviors of the occupant of position one to a great extent. Clearly, the payoffs offered to player one orient him toward a preference for coalitions with the occupant of the number two position. Since player one's maximizing strategy is to select player number five with a probability of .76 and player number two with a probability of only .24, it is clear that the structure in which the interactions take place exerts a considerable effect on player one's behavior.

     In addition to predicting the equilibrium point to which a system moves, given a specified set of payoffs available to members, the theory can be used to predict precisely how much a complex interaction system will be affected by changes in the behaviors of one of its members. Consider the chain structure represented in Figure 11.8. Assume that for the occupant of position number four the utilities for alternative coalitions are altered by changing the payoffs that he is offered. In the altered situation, player four is offered 10 cents for a coalition with player number five and five cents for a coalition with player number three. The effect on the equilibrium behavior of the interaction system is to move to the point described in the matrix in Figure 11.10. The entries in this matrix are the probabilities with which individuals in the row positions will choose the players in the column positions ($P_{x,y}$).

Individual chosen (Y)

		One	Two	Three	Four	Five
	One		.46			.54
	Two	.21		.79		
Individual choosing (X)	Three		.79		.21	
	Four			.46		.54
	Five	.50			.50	

Figure 11.10

It is interesting to consider the interaction patterns that emerge in the structure described by the matrix in Figure 11.10. The most intriguing aspect of the model's prediction is that players two and three enter into a strong alliance. They choose one another with probabilities of .79. Although due to payoff considerations it might be expected that players one and two, and four and three, would develop strong alliances, this is not the case. The strategies that maximize utility with respect to the behaviors of all other members of the system are as specified above.

The effect of the changed reward structure on the equilibrium behavior of the system can be most easily shown by presenting the information reported in Figure 11.9 in matrix form (see Figure 11.11) and making a direct comparison between matrices.

The effects of the change in payoff structure can be specified from Figure 11.11 by subtracting comparable entries in the first matrix from those in the second. The result is reported in Figure 11.12.

The average absolute difference in the behavior of the system is .20.[5] The effect on the occupants of particular positions can be observed by referring to the matrix in Figure 11.12. Observe that although the payoffs offered to the occupant of position five are unchanged, the maximizing

---

5. A convenient measure of the effect of a different payoff structure on the entire system is simply the mean of the absolute differences in the behaviors of the occupants of equivalent structural positions. The variance of the distribution of differences provides a measure of how the effect of the difference in payoff structure is distributed throughout the system.

First payoff structure

Y

	One	Two	Three	Four	Five
One		.24			.76
Two	.12		.88		
X Three		.67		.33	
Four			.67		.33
Five	.87			.13	

Second payoff structure

Y

	One	Two	Three	Four	Five
One		.46			.54
Two	.21		.79		
X Three		.79		.21	
Four			.46		.54
Five	.50			.50	

Figure 11.11

Y

	One	Two	Three	Four	Five
One		+.22			-.22
Two	+.09		-.09		
X Three		+.12		-.12	
Four			-.21		+.21
Five	-.37			+.37	

Figure 11.12

strategy for player five is most affected by the change in the payoffs offered to player four. Using the procedure outlined above it would be possible to consider the effects of any possible change in the payoffs offered to members of the system. In this fashion it would be possible to determine, for example, the optimal change to introduce in order to produce some desired effect on the system.

II. INTERACTION NETWORKS

Consider an interaction structure of the type represented in Figure 11.13, a seven-position interaction network. In terms of its properties, a network differs from a chain in only one major way. In structures defined as networks it is possible for a path to leave and return to its point of origin in more than two steps without passing through all the positions in the structure and without passing through the same point twice. In chain structures it is necessary to pass through all positions in the system. This property of a structure has an effect on the degree to which a change in the behavior of one member of the system will affect the equilibrium behaviors of individuals who occupy other positions in the system.

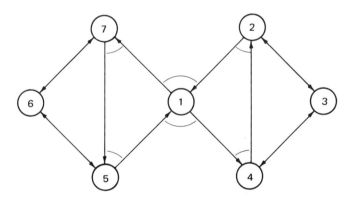

Figure 11.13 *A Seven-Position Interaction Network.*

The communication channels represented in Figure 11.13 reveal a variation in the structure of interactions between system members that has not been permitted in the systems considered previously. Note that position one is related to four other positions in the network. The decision problem for the occupant of position one is to predict when he is going to be chosen by the occupants of positions two and five. If he correctly predicts when these two players are going to select him, he receives some predetermined payoff. The

manner in which the interactions between members of the system are structured is such that if the occupant of position one selects the number five
player on some trial it is communicated to players in the number four and
seven positions as a choice of player number four. For cases other than the
usual symmetric communication channel between positions, the relationship
between inputs to a position and how outputs from that position are communicated to related positions are shown by bonds between appropriate
directed lines.

Permitting positions to be interrelated in the manner described above
introduces a new variety to the types of possible interactions between system
members. Consider the decision problem confronting the occupant of the
number one position. He must attempt to coordinate his behaviors to those
of players two and five. Since for both of these individuals it is the case that
their payoffs are not dependent on predicting player one's outputs, player
one has no power to influence either individual in the usual sense. Player one's
problem calls for adjusting his decision strategy to that of players two and
five, in the same manner as if he were a subordinate in an organization and
forced to adjust his behavior to the outputs of two superiors.

The analogy between the system represented in Figure 11.13 and the
structure of a hierarchically organized system is not entirely appropriate
(and was not intended to be), since player one can indirectly influence the
individuals with whose behaviors he must coordinate his decision strategy.
Observe that player one is in direct interaction with player number seven, and
player seven is in direct interaction with the occupant of position number
five. Since player one's decision strategy will affect player seven's behavior
and his behavior will affect the occupant of the number five position, player
one has an indirect effect on the behavior of player number five. The system
could, of course, be restructured into a hierarchical form and the theory
applied to problems of how power and influence are exercised in structures
of this type.

The network represented in Figure 11.13 is composed of positions that
are related to other positions in the network in three distinct fashions. Some
positions are directly related to two other positions through the usual type of
symmetric communication channel (i.e., positions three and six). Some positions are related to one other position through the usual symmetric communication channel and to a second position through a channel that permits
only limited influence to be applied (i.e., positions two, four, five, and seven).
Finally, one position is related to two other positions through channels that
permit only limited influence (i.e., position one). The differences in relations
between positions in the structure in no way prevents application of the
generalized decision model.

Assume that participants in a system with a structure identical to the one

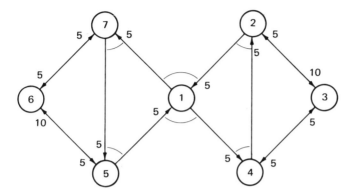

Figure 11.14 *An Interaction Network with Payoffs to Players.*

presented in Figure 11.13 were offered payoffs for alternative coalitions in the manner specified in Figure 11.14.

Given this payoff structure, the behavior of the system can be described in the usual fashion. Solution of the equations that describe the system yield a prediction for its equilibrium point that is reported in the matrix in Figure 11.15.

In addition to predicting the degree to which the equilibrium point of the system will be affected by a change in the payoffs offered to any subset of system members, the model may be employed in order to analyze the relative structurally determined power available to occupants of various positions in the structure. For example, it is possible to determine the degree to which the

Individual chosen (Y)

		One	Two	Three	Four	Five	Six	Seven
	One				.50			.50
	Two	.47		.53				
	Three		.82		.18			
Individual choosing (X)	Four		.78	.22				
	Five	.47					.53	
	Six					.82		.18
	Seven					.78	.22	

Figure 11.15

occupant of position one can affect the behaviors of all other members of the system, given some specified change in his payoffs for alternative choices. The degree to which the system is affected by the same change in the payoffs offered to the occupant of position number two can also be determined. Any difference in the extent to which the system is affected by identical changes in payoffs offered to occupants of different positions must be a function of the location of the positions within the social structure.

The manner in which influence will be transmitted through a complex network is by no means obvious and certainly the precise effects of a given change in the factors affecting the occupant of a particular position cannot be specified on an intuitive basis. Consider the structure of the network under discussion. Position number one *appears* to be the most structurally powerful position in the system, since player number one is in the only position which can introduce influence directly into the two major subdivisions of the network. Position one would be identified as being at a transfer point between the two subdivisions of the structure and, since there is no well-developed theory of how influence is transmitted through complex systems, would very likely be identified as the inherently most powerful position in the network. Analysis of the structure of the network will reveal that this is not true.

In order to clearly analyze the structural power of positions in the network a baseline condition must be established against which the effects of identical changes in the payoffs offered to occupants of different positions can be measured. The ideal baseline against which to contrast the effects of any change is to obtain a description of the system's equilibrium point when every position occupant is offered five cents for each of his alternative coalitions. Under these conditions the maximizing strategy for each member of the system is to distribute his choices with a probability of one-half for each alternative. If the payoffs offered to only one of the system members are altered and he is offered 10 cents for forming one coalition and five cents for the other, it is possible to estimate the effects on the system by solving for the new equilibrium point and calculating the difference between each player's baseline condition maximizing strategy and his strategy given the altered payoffs. Table 11.6 summarizes the effects of changing the payoffs offered to occupants of selected positions in the system.

The absolute differences in choice strategies reported in Table 11.6 indicate the degree to which the maximizing strategies of occupants of each position in the system are affected by changes in the payoffs offered to one member. Since the payoffs are identical in every case, any difference in results must be a function of the manner in which the target position is related to the remainder of the network. Observe that the effects on the system are not equal with equivalent changes in the payoffs for occupants of all positions. The mean absolute change in the system induced by changing only the payoffs offered to the occupant of position number one is .10. Identical changes in the payoffs offered to occupants of either position six or seven produce somewhat lesser effects on the system (for position six $|\bar{x}| = .06$; for position seven $|\bar{x}| = .07$). In terms of its relative structural power, position number one does not possess the greatest inherent ability to influence the system. Given the sample of possible changes for which effects were calculated, the analysis demonstrates that position five possesses the greatest degree of structurally determined power. The mean absolute effect of the system is a .14 difference in the maximizing strategies of occupants of positions in the structure.

Table 11.6 *Absolute Effects of Changes in Payoffs from Baseline to Test Conditions*

Position affecting*	Position affected							$|\bar{X}|$	s^2
	One	Two	Three	Four	Five	Six	Seven		
One	—	.07	.07	.15	.07	.07	.15	.10	.002
Four	.05	.08	.08	—	.03	.03	.07	.06	.001
Five	.04	.02	.02	.05	—	.35	.34	.14	.026
Six	.01	.01	.01	.02	.02	—	.28	.06	.012
Seven	.06	.04	.04	.09	.11	.11	—	.08	.001

*The payoffs for alternative coalitions for the position under examination were assigned as follows: $P_{1,2}$ = \$.05, $P_{1,5}$ = \$.10; $P_{4,1}$ = \$.10, $P_{4,3}$ = \$.05; $P_{5,6}$ = \$.05, $P_{5,7}$ = \$.10; $P_{6,5}$ = \$.05, $P_{6,7}$ = \$.10; $P_{7,1}$ = \$.10, $P_{7,6}$ = \$.05.

The structural power of a position can be considered in a second manner. Calculating the mean absolute effect on the system provides a measure of the gross power of a position, but does not fully describe the extent to which the occupant of a position affects the behavior of the other members of the system. The variance of the mean effect provides a measure of the manner in which structural power is dispersed throughout the system. The variances in the mean effects of changes in payoffs available to position occupants are reported in Table 11.6. When structural power is considered in this fashion, the results indicate that positions number one, four, and seven have a quite consistent effect on the system in the sense that all players are affected to nearly the same degree when changes are initiated through these positions in the network. Compare, for example, the manner in which the changes in payoffs offered to player one affect the entire system with the effects of a similar alteration in the payoffs offered to player number five. Although position number five possesses the greatest absolute mean structural power, the position's power is largely restricted to those positions to which position five is directly related. Position five has only a minimal effect on positions that are more than one step removed in the structure. For position one, the effects on the system are quite different. There are substantial changes in the maximizing strategies of all members of the system.

11.3 CONCLUSION

It is a virtually hopeless task to attempt any satisfactory final summary statement of the work that precedes this sentence. This task is made exceedingly difficult for two reasons. First, it is obvious from the immediately preceding sections that experimental work following from this decision theory is not at an end. Second, since the theoretical and experimental work reported herein deal with the formulation and evaluation of a theory that postulates rational behavior with respect to human goals, the important aspects of the work are intimately related to economics and most of the major questions in the social sciences. The facet of this research that we regard as most significant is that it contributes to a major theoretical tradition at both the analytic and empirical levels and leads directly to the application of the theory to a number of important issues.

Appendix I:
Estimation of Alpha
Ratios from More
than Minimal Data

The discussion of the method used for estimation of utility ratios from more than minimum data follows Siegel's development of the method as presented in *Choice, Strategy and Utility*, Chapter 5 and the Appendix. The presentation and method have been slightly modified for the particular conditions of the research reported in this book.

In the event that experimental procedures yield more than the minimum data necessary to estimate utility parameters, the situation may be described by the following set of equations:

$$
\begin{aligned}
\alpha_1\pi_1 - \alpha_2\pi_2 &= 4(P_1 - .5) \\
\alpha_1\pi_1' - \alpha_2\pi_2' &= 4(P_1' - .5) \\
&\cdots\cdots\cdots\cdots\cdots\cdots \\
\alpha_1\pi_1^{(K)} - \alpha_2\pi_2^{(K)} &= 4(P_1^{(K)} - .5)
\end{aligned}
\tag{A1}
$$

where $K \geq 2$.

The two unknowns of the equations are α_1 and α_2. The problem is to obtain a single solution to the overdetermined set of K equations with two unknowns. It is the case, however, that the K hyperplanes defined by the K equations may not have a common point of intersection and therefore the K equations will not have a solution. This situation results from a sampling difference between the observed stable-state choice probabilities and the true choice probabilities rather than from an inadequacy of the model. The model specifies only that the K equations will have a solution for the true choice probabilities.

Since there may be no values for α_1 and α_2 which will satisfy all K equations, Siegel devised a method for obtaining an approximate solution, such that the sum of the squares of the Euclidean distances from the point $\alpha = (\alpha_1, \alpha_2)$ to each of the hyperplanes is minimal.[1]

The system of K equations obtained from the experimental conditions may be written as:

$$\sum_{i=1}^{2} A_{gi}\alpha_i = B_g \qquad g = 1, 2 \ldots, K \tag{A2}$$

Let $\epsilon_g(\alpha^0)$ denote the distance of the point $\alpha^0 = (\alpha_1^0, \alpha_2^0)$ from the hyperplane $\sum_{i=1}^{2} A_{gi}\alpha_i = B_g$. It may be seen that

$$\epsilon_g(\alpha^0) = \frac{\left| B_g - \sum_{i=1}^{2} A_{gi}\alpha_i^0 \right|}{C_g}$$

where $C_g = \sqrt{\sum_{i=1}^{2} A_{gi}^2}$.

The quantity $\sum_{g=1}^{K} \epsilon_g^2$ is minimized when

$$\frac{\partial}{\partial \alpha_h} \sum_{g=1}^{K} \frac{\left(B_g - \sum_{i=1}^{2} A_{gi}\alpha_i \right)^2}{C_g^2} = 0 \qquad h = 1, 2$$

From the above expression the following system of equations is obtained.

$$\sum_{i=1}^{2} \left(\sum_{g=1}^{K} \frac{A_{gi}A_{gh}}{C_g^2} \right) \alpha_i = \sum_{g=1}^{K} \frac{B_g A_{gh}}{C_g^2} \qquad h = 1, 2 \tag{A3}$$

1. The method employed here differs from the usual least squares procedure in which the distance from a point is measured as oblique rather than orthogonal to the hyperplane.

Equations (A2) can be written in matrical form as

$$A\alpha' = B$$

where A is the $K \times 2$ matrix of the A_{gi}'s, α' is the 2×1 matrix of α_i's, and B is the $K \times 1$ matrix of B_g's.

Equations (A3) can be written matrically as

$$A'CA\alpha' = A'CB$$

where C is the $K \times K$ diagonal matrix with diagonal elements C_g^{-2}. Then the set of α_i's which solve Eq. (A3) is given by the 2×1 matrix

$$\alpha' = (A'CA)^{-1}A'CB \qquad (A4)$$

The method outlined above may be applied to the data from Experiment V in order to estimate α_1 and α_2 under unequal alpha experimental conditions. Starting with the set of overdetermined equations

$$\pi_1\alpha_1 - \pi_2\alpha_2 = 4(P_1 - .5)$$
$$\pi_1'\alpha_1 - \pi_2'\alpha_2 = 4(P_1' - .5)$$
$$\pi_1''\alpha_1 - \pi_2''\alpha_2 = 4(P_1'' - .5)$$

the stable-state choice probabilities observed in Experiment V may be introduced:

$$.8\alpha_1 - .2\alpha_2 = 4(.671605 - .5) \quad \text{(Condition } G)$$
$$.7\alpha_1 - .3\alpha_2 = 4(.539286 - .5) \quad \text{(Condition } C)$$
$$.6\alpha_1 - .4\alpha_2 = 4(.439744 - .5) \quad \text{(Condition } H)$$

The solution for α_1 and α_2 can be obtained using Eq. (A4):

$$\hat{\alpha}_1 = (A'CA)^{-1}(A'CB)$$

The matrices A, B, and C are:

$$A = \begin{bmatrix} \pi_1 - \pi_2 \\ \pi_1' - \pi_2' \\ \pi_1'' - \pi_2'' \end{bmatrix} = \begin{bmatrix} .8 & -.2 \\ .7 & -.3 \\ .6 & -.4 \end{bmatrix}$$

$$B = \begin{bmatrix} 4(P_1 - .5) \\ 4(P_1' - .5) \\ 4(P_1'' - .5) \end{bmatrix} = \begin{bmatrix} 4(.671605 - .5) \\ 4(.539286 - .5) \\ 4(.439744 - .5) \end{bmatrix}$$

$$C = \begin{bmatrix} C_1^{-2} & 0 & 0 \\ 0 & C_2^{-2} & 0 \\ 0 & 0 & C_3^{-2} \end{bmatrix} = \begin{bmatrix} \dfrac{1}{.68} & 0 & 0 \\ 0 & \dfrac{1}{.58} & 0 \\ 0 & 0 & \dfrac{1}{.52} \end{bmatrix}$$

From these matrices, the following can be computed:

$$A'CA = \begin{bmatrix} 2.47831 & -1.05890 \\ -1.05890 & .52169 \end{bmatrix}$$

$$(A'CA)^{-1} = \begin{bmatrix} 3.03955 & 6.16956 \\ 6.16956 & 14.43958 \end{bmatrix}$$

$$A'CB = \begin{bmatrix} .71910 \\ -.09777 \end{bmatrix}$$

The estimate can be obtained using these matrices and Eq. (A4):

$$\hat{\alpha}' = \begin{bmatrix} 1.58258 & 3.02485 \end{bmatrix}$$

Using the data from Experiment I, estimates for α under equal payoff conditions can be obtained in an analogous manner.

Appendix II: Data

The raw data from all experiments together with the series of robot choices for the robot-interactive experiments are reported in this appendix.

The data from the robot-interactive experiments are organized to correspond with the presentation in the text. Subjects are always player number three, and hence their choices are reported as a string of ones and twos. A one choice indicates a selection of robot one and a two indicates a selection of robot two. The robot number corresponds to π terms in the text. Robot $1 = \pi_1$. When $\pi_1 = .70$ robot one chose the subject with a probability of .70.

The data from the free-interactive games are also reported in a manner compatible with the text. Subjects playing from position number one make choices of either player two or three, etc.

ROBOT CHOICES

The series of robot choices for all of the treatment conditions are reported below. A zero (0) indicates a trial on which the subject *was not* chosen by the robot. A one (1) indicates a trial on which the subject *was chosen.*

$\pi = .80$

011111101111011111101011110111111111110011110011111
011111101111011111101011110111111111110011110011111

$\pi = .20$

100010000000001000010100100000000000110000010001000
100010000000001000010100100000000000110000010001000

$\pi = .70$

011011101111011011101011110101111101100111110011110
011011101111011011101011110101111101100111110011110

$\pi = .30$

100110000000001100010100100010000010110000010011001
100110000000001100010100100010000010110000010011001

$\pi = .60$

010011101110111010010011111001110101110000111100011
010011101110111010010011111001110101110000111100011

$\pi = .40$

100110010011000101001000100110010010001101000001110
100110010011000101001000100110010010001101000001110

CONDITION A

Trials 1 . . . 100   Subject

```
2222221111111111111111111111111111111111111111111111     1
1221111111111111111111111111111111111111111222211111111

2112111212221211111212211212121122112112111111211111     2
1111122211111112122111211111111121111112112211112211111

2122121111111111111111111111111111111111111111111111     3
1111111111111111111111111111111111111111111111111111

2112212212222121112111111111111111111112122222111111111     4
1221222111111111122212222222111111111122222222111111111

2221111111111111111112111111111221111111112111112121111     5
1111111112111111111111111111111111111111111111111111111

2222221222222212112111211212121222111111112211111111     6
1112112221111111111111111111111111122111111111111111111

2221222221111121112112121111111111111111111211112211     7
1111112111112112222111111111111111222222221111111111

1111111121111111111111111111112111111111111111111111     8
1211111111111111111111111111111111111111111111111111

2212122122111211111112121111112111111111121111111111     9
2221222111111111111111111111111111111111111111111111

2121111121222121222211222111111121111121122222122111     10
1221111111111121121111121111111111111122222221111111111

2212221122211212212111121111121121111222211122211111     11
2211211121111211211111122111111111111121111111111111

1122211122221111211121111111222111111111111111221211     12
2211121111111111111122211111111111111121111221111

1221222221111111111111111111111111111111111111111111     13
1111111111111111111111111111122111111222211111111

2221122111111121121111111111121111111111121111121111     14
1111122111111111111112111111111111111111111111111

1221111122111111221122211211111111111111111111111211     15
1111111111111111111111121111111111111111111111111

2221222111111111111111111111111111111111111111111111     16
1111111111111111111111111111111111111111111111111

2222122112111111211111211211111111112222111111121     17
1221111112111111111111121111111111111111111222222
```

112212222111121221221212211211221111222112211111111   18
221121122211121221112211221121122112121121121111221

212211222111111111111111111111111111111111111111111   19
111111111111111111111111111111111111111111111111111

122122212111111111111111111111111111111111111122222   20
222222111111122221112221111111111111111111111122221

222222212222111121111111111111111111111111111111111   21
121111111111111111111111111111111111111111111111111

121111111111111111111111111111111111111111111111111   22
111111111111111111111111111111111111111111111111111

CONDITION A′

Trials 1 . . . 100   Subject

112112111111121121111112111111112111111122111111211111   1
121122111111111112111212112121112111111122221111211211

222222222111111121111111111111111111111111111111111   2
111111111111111111111111111111111111111111111111111

222222112111112222111111111111111111111111111111111   3
111222222111111111111111111111111111111111111111111

121112211111111111111111111111111111111111111221111   4
121111111111111111111112111111111111111122111111111

211211222221111122212221122222111111111111111222111   5
222111111111111111111111111111111111111111111111111

222211221111111111111111111111111111111112222211111111   6
111111111111111111111111121111111111111111111111111

CONDITION B

Trials 1 . . . 100 Subject

```
2222212211222122112221112212212211112221222111112  2    1
2121112212222112211211111212222112221211212211122211

2122212112222222222222222222222222222212222222222222  2
2222222221111212222121122111111111111111111111111122

2222122111111111111112122111111111111222111221111111222  3
2121112221111111122111211111212111111111111111111111111

2222222122222222122211111122221111111111111111222111111112  4
1111112111111111111111111111111111111111111112222211222

2222112222221112222222222222222222222222222221122222221  5
1112112211221222222221121122211222221122211111222111

2222212122111111111112222111122111112111122221111222  6
1111111122112111111121221111112222222111222211111222

1122111212211112111111111112112212121111221111112221  7
1111211111221121121111111111122111111112111111121221

1222222111112222211211111111111111111111111111111111222  8
22222222211111111111111111111112211111121111111111111

1122221112121221222221111112211112111212122222211122221  9
1112222121111111111222211121211221121121111111121112211

1222222221211222211122221211112211221111121222211  10
12221212221221211222112221112112221221111112122211

11221111111111111112222211111121112111111112211111112  11
2211111121111111121111222111112111111111112122222222

2222222222111111211222221111111111112211111121111111  12
111111111112211121111111121112111111111112222111121

1122222211212111222222212221112111212222222211121221  13
2222112222211112221222111121211112111221121112221221

2111121212211222211211122221211121221111111222111112  14
2112222111111111122212222122211121221111121211111212

2222222111111111111112121111111211111211111121111111221  15
1112111121111111121111111112112121111111111111121111121

1111111111111111112112211111112211111111112222211111  16
22222111111111111111122222211212111122222222222111111

111111111111121111211111111111111111121112111111122211  17
1111111111111121112111112211111111121111111111122111
```

```
1222222111111221111211112222111111111221111121111221        18
1211111221112221111111111111112111112112211111122211

1222221111111221121111111112212211111121111112211111122        19
1112221111111111111111222221112121111111111122111222

1111122121111122222222111112221111222122111112222211        20
1111111221111122222221112222111111111122111111122221

2221222111121111111112111111211112112112111112121212121        21
212121212121212121212212121212121212211221122111111222
```

Trials 1 . . . 100   Subject

```
2222221111111111111222211111111111111111122221111111        1
12111111111111111111111111121111111111111111121112222

1222222221111111111111122111111111111111112122211121        2
12112111111111111111111111111112212222211111121111122

1121122222111111222111221111221112222111111122111222        3
1111111221121112211222211112222111121111221111111222

1221222122111111111111111111111111111111111111111111        4
11111111111111111111111111111111111111111111111111111

1122212222222111222222111111122221111111122222222222        5
11111111111122222111122111111221112211112111111111211

1112221122222122212222222221121111111111111121111222        6
2211111121112111211121111111111112111111111111112222

2222221111112221111222221111111211111111111221111122        7
11112221111112221111111111111111111111111112222221122

1211122111111211111112222111111122222121111111111111222        8
2211111121122111211111221122222211221111222111121222

1112112121111221111111112111111121221122211111211211        9
12111211222221212111112121121111222111222211111111111
```

CONDITION C

Trials 1 . . . 100   Subject

11222122222111212121211221212122211121222211111111221   1
22212211111111112221111222211111111122112222111112211

11122211221122122112112212222121122112211221121122 1   2
12121221112211111221112222121112221111121111211122

11111222222211212211111222221111111111111222221221211   3
22211111111122222222222222221212112222111222222221211

22222221122222222222222222222222222222222222222222222   4
22222222222222112222222222222222222222222222222222222

22111221122111222211112222121212222121211221111212222   5
22112222121112112211211211121211112122112111222122

22121222211111111222222222222222122222222222122222222   6
22222222222211122221212222221211111111221111111211

22221212222211211211211211111211222211111112112111111   7
11112211121111111111111121111212112111111111112111112

22222222111111112211111111122211111111112222211111111   8
11111111111111111111111122222211111111111111111111111

12222221221111112211111222222211222111111111111122   9
11111112222222222222121121111111111111111222111111

12221211121111212221122221111122221111121111122111 1   10
22112211111111122211212112111111111111111111211211

22221222211222212221222222112121222211221221222222122   11
11222222222221222212122221221122221221221221121111

21222222221112222111212111111111111212222111221211   12
22222222211111122112111111212211112122211111221111

22212212111111211222222221212122211111122111112212 21   13
22222222222111111221122221222122221121212211111111

22222121111122211222222222221112222111112222111111222   14
21111222222221112211222222221111111121211111111211222

Data

CONDITION C′

Trials 1 . . . 100   Subject

```
1111222122211111222222221212221122211111111111122          1
2222222222222211111112221111111111221222221111111111

2221221212221112221212122221212221112122212112212         2
2212122222111111211121211211121111111112221112221211

1122222222111211121111111122112111111121111122111111         3
1112211221222112112111112212121111111111111111111211

2221221221122222212211112222111222211111221122221122         4
1211222211122111211222212211111222222221112222112112

1121222222111212221121211122222211111212211122211222         5
2211222221111222222221111112222211222212221112211211

1111222111111222222121211112222221122221121122222222         6
2211221121111222222212122222221111111122222111222211

2222221111221112222221111111222212112112111112221222         7
2222222222111111222112222222111112222122111122221212

1122222122212212222212122222221222111212122222222121         8
1222212222212221212211221222222222221212122222221212
```

CONDITION D

Trials 1 . . . 100   Subject

2122211222122112211111222111121222111111112111121112   1
2222211221111111122111112221111111111121111121111111

2221112111211212221111221221111221111221111222111   2
2221111122211111221122211112211122221111111112222111

1111221122111121111121111112111111111112111111211211   3
1111221121111122111111111122111111111121111111111111111

2121222112121121212122121211212121212121212121211211   4
2111211211221112211121211111111221212111112222222221

1111111111111111211111111111111221111111222111111111   5
1222221111111111111111111111111111111111111111111111

1222222111111122211111111221211111222122211122211222   6
2221211122111111221112222111221221121211221112111112

2121212121212112212121211212121212211212121221121212121212   7
1212121212121211221212121212122112121212121212121212

2112112222112212221122111122222111221111122111121   8
2211111222211111221122112122212112222121111221211122

2222211121111211222122211111111122111122111122111   9
2211211111122111111111122111112111122122211111211111

2212221121111211111122211112121111111122111122111   10
2211221111111122211121111111122211121122221121122221

1112211222211111222112211111211111222222211112211112   11
2211111121122211111111111111112222111111111122211112

CONDITION D′

Trials 1 . . . 100   Subject

112221112211221112122222112112222121121112121111 21   1
111112121221111112221111112221212121221111112121111112

112212222112221122111122221122111222122111 22222211   2
221122111112211221112221112222111112212211112222211

212212112211112221122211111222111111122222111111221111   3
111112211111112222111112222112211122221111111111211111

212221211112221122211111122111222211211122111122 1221   4
221111122121112222112211122111112221111111111 2211221

212212121211211212121212112121211221111211121112111121   5
111211211111121112111211112112111112211121111 21111112

211122211122111211122221122111221112212222112222 11211   6
121111121221111122112211111122222111122221121 1211211

CONDITION E

Trials 1 . . . 100   Subject

12222222111111211111122222222222211111221111111 1111111   1
111111111111111111111111111111111111111111111111 111111

212211112111112112211111111121121111111221111211111   2
121111111111111112211112121111111111111211122111111111

112212111212212112211112112111221112211212111 2211122   3
112221111222111221111111211221111222211122221111121

121121111211112212111111221111211111111111111111 221111   4
111111111111211111111111111111111111111111121111111111

1211111111111111111111111221111111111111122222222 11211111   5
111111111111211111111111111111121111112111111111 111111

11111222211111211111111112212111222111111111111 211211   6
121111111111111111111111111111121112121111211111 2111211

1111111111111111111111111111111111111111111111 1111111   7
111111111111111111111111111111111111111111111111 111111

22211222111111111111111111111111221111212222221 1211111   8
222122112111111111111111111111111111111111111 1111111

211221222221212221122121221222111221112221111 121222   9
2211121221111111212121112211121211111111211121 2221122

CONDITION F

Trials 1 . . . 100	Subject

```
1112212221111122112111122122111111111122221122111       1
2122222222222221112212222211111222221111112222112222

1222222221111111111111111111111111111111111111111       2
1111111111122222222222222222222222222222222222222222

2212122211211111111111222111111112211122111111111111    3
1111222222222222222222222222222222222222111112222222

2221212111111111221111112222112111111112222221111111111  4
22222222222222211112222222111222222221111112222222111

2112211111211112111121111111111111111111111111111111    5
1112111111111111111111121222222222222222222222222222

1111211212211111221111112212222211111111221111222211    6
2222111112222222111211122222222222211111122211222222

2221221111111111121111111111111111111111111111111111    7
1122211222222222222222222222222222222222222222222222

1222221111111111111111121122111211121111221112222221    8
1112111111222222212222222221222222222222222222222221

2221221111111111122211111121111111211111111111111111111  9
1112222222222222222222222222222222222222222222222222
```

CONDITION G

Trials 1 . . . 100   Subject

```
2221121111111112111111112111211111111112221111111211          1
1222222221111111111111111111111111111111112221111222221

1222222212111112111112222222122211111112211111211222         2
2222222211111111222212222222111111111111111111111111

2222222111111111121111112222222222111111111111211112         3
2221111121111111111111111111111111122222222222222221

1122222222111212221112222122211112211122111111111221         4
1222222221111121111112112222221111111221221111111212

2221121121111111121111222212111121111111122222211222221      5
1211122222111111221111222212222221111111112221111222211

2222222222222211111111111122221111111111111121111111111      6
1111111111111122211111111111111111111111111111111111111

1122121212222221212222222222222221212121222221222222222      7
1222222121212222211112222222221221122112211221221211

1111111111111111111111111111111111111111111111111111111      8
1111111111111111111111111111111111111111111111111111111

2221121111111111111111111111221111121111111111111111111      9
1222222111111111111112122111111111111111112111111222211
```

CONDITION H

Trials 1 . . . 100	Subject

```
2222221122121221211111222112112222211121222222221212     1
1221122222222111111122222221111111212121212122211122

1112211222222222221112211222111121111212221221112221     2
1211122122222211222221111222122112122222222211222222

2222212212221111111121221111111221221111111222211112     3
2221212122122221211221111222111212211112211222222121

2122122221122221222221122222222212212221222211111222     4
1222221121122211221222221112222211112122222212111122

1122211212211222122221122222212112212111211122222221     5
1222211122221112221222221112112211221211121111221211

2221212122111112221122111111122111122122222112221111     6
1222222221111122121111221221112121111111122121111221

2222122211112211122222112222221211221222211221111221     7
1212111111211112221111222221112112211111211111222212

1222222222122211212222222222222211111111112122111222     8
1211221122112222212212222211111111111111112221111122

1222222222221221121112111111111122111211211112211     9
1222222221111112111112122221111112211221111111112222

2222221212221122222222111222221111112222222222111222     10
1112222111112111212222222211122222221112211211122

2221222212211211112111212221211122111121111121111122     11
2222222212111222122122222212211222221222212222222

2112222211221122112221111222211112111221111222211     12
1112112221112212211111221222111121111122111122111

1112122212212222212222122211222222222222222222222222     13
2222222222222222222222222222222222222222222222222222
```

EXPERIMENT VI

Trials 1 . . . 50	Group	Position

	Group	Position
22222222222222222222222222233322223322222322233322233	1	1
31133333131111111133333333113333111133313333311331113	1	2
11112222122111111112222221122221111112122211122111	1	3
22322222333222232222222222223222233322322332222333	2	1
11111133331331111131113113111311113131131133111133	2	2
12222211111221122221121221111111111111111111111111	2	3
22332233322222322332222232222323323333333322222333	3	1
13131333133311113333333313333331111133333331111111	3	2
11122111111222111112112221211111111111111112222211111	3	3
32233222332222222232222322332223233233232233332232	4	1
33333313333331311333331111333111333333333333333313	4	2
21211121221222111122211111121112221222111122222222	4	3

EXPERIMENT VII—POSITION 1

Trials 1 . . . 60   Subject

2222323233323232323333322223222222233233232223232323   1
2232323232

3223322233223322333322323322333233223323333233232222   2
222222222

2222323232333222333332222322222222222222222222222222   3
222222222

3332322323222323223223232222322223232232322232322333   4
2332323322

3332222322233222222222222222222222222222222222222222   5
222222222

3332223322232222222233223232232222222333222222223222   6
222222222

2222322322222222222222222222222222222222222222222222   7
222222222

3222333333333333333322233223323222222222222222222222   8
222222222

2222222222223322222222333333222222222222222222222222   9
222222222

33322222222333333333222223333333322222222222233333222   10
3333322222

33222332333232222322232322223222222222222222222222222   11
222222222

22222222222222222233222222222222322222232222222222   12
2322222222

2222222222232322233222222222222222222222333333322222   13
222223222222

33322222222222222222222222222222222222222222222222222   14
222222222

EXPERIMENT VII—POSITION 2

Trials 1 . . . 60   Subject

333333333333333333333313333331133133333333333333333   1
3333333333

333333333333333333331333333333333333333333333333111111   2
1111111111

111113133333333333311131111111111111111111111111111   3
1111111111

311333333333333333333333333333333333333333333333333333   4
3333333333

333133313333311111111111111111111111111111111111111111   5
1111111111

311133333333333313333313333331133113333331111133111   6
1111133333

311111111331111111111111111111111111111111111111111   7
1111111111

11333333333333313333333333133111111111111111111111111   8
1111111111

111131111313131111313311111111111111111111111111111111   9
1111111111

1113111111111311131111111133131111111111111331333   10
3333333333

3331333311311313131311111131131311111131133113311331133   11
1313131313

11111111111111111111111111111111111111111111111111111   12
1111111111

11111111133331133333111111331133333333333333111111   13
1113333333

3113111111111111111111111111111111111111111111111111   14
1111111111

EXPERIMENT VII—POSITION 3

Trials 1 . . . 60	Subject
222222222222222222221111222112111222222222222222222 222222222	1
112221222212211222222222211222222222222222222211111111 1111112222	2
112112222112221211112222122111122221212111111121122 222222222	3
222222222222222222222222222222222222222222222222221222 222222222	4
221122112221221222221222221222222122222212222212222 2222211111	5
222222222222222222222222222222222222212222222222111 1111222222	6
21121121211221212211211212212121211211222222222221121 1121122121	7
2221111111111112212121122112222222122212221122222 1111111111	8
21221212222221122212211111112111122221111222211112 2221111222	9
11111112111111111111111211111111111121122221111112 222222222	10
21111122122122111111222222222211111222122222112222 222221212	11
22221221112221211111121112222211112221112111222222 1112121111	12
22112221222212222222222221122222222222222222222122 222222222	13
12111121111222221121222212211111112222222222221111 1121222121	14

References

Berger, J., Cohen, B., Snell, J., and Zelditch, M. *Types of Formalization in Small-Group Research.* Boston: Houghton Mifflin, 1962.

Bixenstine, V., and Blundell, H. Control of choice exerted by structural factors in 2-person, non-zero-sum games. *Journal of Conflict Resolution,* 10, 1966, 478–87.

Bixenstine, V., Potash, H., and Wilson, K. Effects of level of cooperative choice by the other player on choices in a Prisoner's Dilemma Game. Part I. *Journal of Abnormal and Social Psychology,* 66, 1963, 308–13.

Bixenstine, V., and Wilson, K. Effects of level of cooperative choice by the other player on choices in a Prisoner's Dilemma Game. Part II. *Journal of Abnormal and Social Psychology,* 67, 1963, 139–47.

Bond, J. R., and Vinacke, W. E. Coalitions in mixed-sex triads. *Sociometry,* 24, 1961, 61–74.

Caplow, T. A. *Two Against One: Coalitions in Triads.* Englewood Cliffs, N. J.: Prentice-Hall, Inc., 1968.

Caplow, T. A. A theory of coalitions in the triad. *American Sociological Review,* 21, 1956, 489–93.

Cartwright, D., and Harary, F. Structural balance: a generalization of Heider's theory. *Psychological Review*, 63, 1956, 277–93.

Chaney, M. V., and Vinacke, W. E. Achievement and nurturance in the triad. *Journal of Abnormal and Social Psychology*, 60, 1960, 175–81.

Chertkoff, J. M. A revision of Caplow's coalition theory. *Journal of Experimental Social Psychology*, 3, 1967, 172–77.

Chertkoff, J. M. The effects of probability of future success on coalition formation. *Journal of Experimental Social Psychology*, 2, 1966, 265–77.

Cohen, B. *Conflict and Conformity*. Cambridge, Mass.: Technology Press, 1963.

Deutsch, M. The effects of motivational orientation on trust and suspicion. *Human Relations*, 13, 1960, 123–39.

Deutsch, M. Trust and suspicion. *Journal of Conflict Resolution*, 2, 1958, 265–79.

Emerson, R. M. Power-dependence relations: two experiments. *Sociometry*, 27, 1964, 282–98.

Festinger, L. A theory of social comparison processes. *Human Relations*, 7, 1954, 117–40.

Gallo, P., and McClintock, C. Cooperative and competitive behavior in mixed-motives games. *Journal of Conflict Resolution*, 9, 1965, 68–78.

Gamson, W. A. Experimental studies of coalition formation. In *Advances in Experimental Social Psychology* (L. Berkowitz, ed.). Vol. I. New York: Academic Press, 1964.

Gamson, W. A. An experimental test of a theory of coalition formation. *American Sociological Review*, 26, 1961, 565–73.

Goodnow, J. J. Determinants of choice-distribution in two-choice situations. *American Journal of Psychology*, 68, 1955, 106–16.

Humphreys, L. G. Acquisition and extinction of verbal expectations in a situation analogous to conditioning. *Journal of Experimental Psychology*, 25, 1939, 294–301.

Jonckheere, A. R. A distribution-free *k*-sample test against ordered alternatives. *Biometrika*, 41, 1954, 133–45.

Kalisch, G. K., Milner, J. W., Nash, J. F., and Nering, E. D. Some experimental *n*-person games. In *Decision Processes* (R. M. Thrall, C. H. Coombs, and R. L. Davis, eds.). New York: Wiley, 1954.

Kelley, H. H., and Arrowood, A. J. Coalitions in the triad: critique and experiment. *Sociometry*, 23, 1960, 231–44.

Lave, L. Factors affecting cooperation in the Prisoner's Dilemma. *Behavioral Science*, 10, 1965, 26–38.

Lerner, M. J., and Becker, S. Interpersonal choice as a function of ascribed similarity and definition of the situation. *Human Relations*, 15, 1962, 27–34.

Lieberman, B. Experimental studies of conflict in some two-person games. In *Mathematical Methods in Small Group Processes* (J. Criswell, H. Solomon, and P. Suppes, eds.). Stanford: Stanford University Press, 1962.

Loomis, J. Communication, the development of trust and cooperative behavior. *Human Relations*, 12, 1959, 305–15.

Luce, R. D., and Raiffa, H. *Games and Decisions*. New York: Wiley, 1957.

Lutzker, R. Internationalism as a predictor of cooperative behavior. *Journal of Conflict Resolution*, 4, 1960, 426–30.

McClintock, C., Harrison, A., Strand, S., and Gallo, P. Internationalism-Isolationism, strategy of the other player and 2-person game behavior. *Journal of Abnormal and Social Psychology*, 67, 1963, 631–36.

Messick, M., and Thorngate, W. Relative gain maximization in experimental games. *Journal of Experimental Social Psychology*, 3, 1967, 85–101.

Mills, T. M. Power relations in three-person groups. *American Sociological Review*, 18, 1953, 351–57.

Minas, J., Scodel, A., Marlowe, D., and Rawson, H. Some descriptive aspects of 2-person, non-zero-sum games. Part II. *Journal of Conflict Resolution*, 4, 1960, 193–97.

Oskamp, S., and Perlam, D. Factors affecting cooperation in a Prisoner's Dilemma Game. *Journal of Conflict Resolution*, 9, 1965, 359–74.

Radlow, R. An experimental study of cooperation in the Prisoner's Dilemma Game. *Journal of Conflict Resolution*, 9, 1965, 221–27.

Rapoport, A., and Chammah, A. *Prisoner's Dilemma*. Ann Arbor: University of Michigan Press, 1965.

Scodel, A. Induced collaboration in some non-zero-sum games. *Journal of Conflict Resolution*, 6, 1962, 335–40.

Scodel, A., Minas, J., Ratoosh, P., and Lipetz, M. Some descriptive aspects of two-person non-zero-sum games. *Journal of Conflict Resolution*, 3, 1959, 114–19.

Shure, G., and Meeker, R. Empirical demonstration of normative behavior in the prisoner's dilemma. *Proceedings*, 76th Annual Convention, APA, 1968.

Siegel, S., Siegel, A. E., and Andrews, J. M. *Choice, Strategy and Utility*. New York: McGraw-Hill, 1964.

Siegel, S., and Goldstein, D. A. Decision-making behavior in a two-choice uncertain outcome situation. *Journal of Experimental Psychology*, 57, 1959, 37–42.

Simmel, G. *The Sociology of George Simmel* (translated and edited by Kurt Wolff). Glencoe, Ill.: The Free Press, 1950.

Stinchcombe, A. *Constructing Social Theories*. New York: Harcourt, Brace & World, 1968.

Strodtbeck, F. L. The family as a three-person group. *American Sociological Review*, 19, 1954, 23–29.

Stryker, S., and Psathas, G. Research on coalitions in the triad—findings, problems, and strategy. *Sociometry*, 23, 1960, 217–30.

Uesugi, T. K., and Vinacke, W. E. Strategy in a feminine game. *Sociometry*, 26, 1963, 75–88.

Vinacke, W. E. The effect of cumulative score on coalition formation in triads with various patterns of internal power. *American Psychologist*, 14, 1959*a*, 381.

Vinacke, W. E. Sex roles in a three-person game. *Sociometry*, 22, 1959*b*, 343–60.

Vinacke, W. E., and Arkoff, A. An experimental study of coalitions in the triad. *American Sociological Review*, 22, 1957, 406–14.

Vinacke, W. E., Crowell, D. C., Dien, D., and Young, V. The effect of information about strategy on a three-person game. *Behavioral Science*, 11, 1966, 180–89.

Vinacke, W. E., and Gullickson, G. R. Age and sex differences in the formation of coalitions. *Child Development*, 35, 1964, 1217–31.

Von Neumann, J., and Morgenstern, O. *Theory of Games and Economic Behavior*. Princeton, N. J.: Princeton University Press, 1944.

Willis, R. H. Coalitions in the tetrad. *Sociometry*, 25, 1962, 358–76.

Wilson, W., Chun, N., and Ratayani, M. *Projection, Attraction, and Strategy Choices in Intergroup Competition*. University of Hawaii, 1964. Mimeographed.

Author Index

197

Subject Index